Five Generations

Benjamin B. Brown, Alexander S. Brown, Dora E. (Brown) Hoitt
William Brown, Clarence B. Hoitt

THE DESCENDANTS

OF

WILLIAM BROWN
(1819–1908)

AND

ISABELLA KENNEDY
(1820–1894)

of
Ireland, Scotland, and
Hampton Falls, New Hampshire

Wilma T. Regan &
Laird C. Towle

HERITAGE BOOKS
2026

HERITAGE BOOKS

AN IMPRINT OF HERITAGE BOOKS, INC.

Books, CDs, and more—Worldwide

For our listing of thousands of titles see our website
at
www.HeritageBooks.com

A Facsimile Reprint
Published 2026 by
HERITAGE BOOKS, INC.
Publishing Division
5810 Ruatan Street
Berwyn Heights, MD 20740

International Standard Book Number
Paperbound: 978-1-55613-028-1

This genealogy is
dedicated to

Clyde Lind (Brown) Bussell
&
Maude Aileen Brown

who both
inspired its creation
and
contributed extensively
to its contents

CONTENTS

PREFACE

The compilation of a family history is a work of love. It involves much patient searching and careful assembling of bits and pieces of data. To many this appears mere drudgery and dissuades them from recording the history of their family; but to those who have been bitten by the "genealogical bug" each new discovery is a thrill, and rediscovering the lives of their ancestors provides great satisfaction.

Some people are chagrined at the fallibility of their ancestors and seem to demand a much higher standard of morality and ethics from them than they require of themselves. That sort of unrealistic attitude fills closets with skeletons and makes family research unnecessarily difficult. We subscribe to the words of Thomas Fuller who said *"He without beggars, fools, knaves or thieves in his family was begat by a flash of lightning."* In preparing this history we have attempted to portray the families honestly, but without dwelling on some of their scandalous escapades.

Preparation of this history began in the summer of 1969 with extensive correspondence with many members of the family soliciting their cooperation in providing data on their family lines. Many responded most generously for which we are grateful. After that preliminary stage we began researching in old newspapers, wills, deeds, census records, etc. in order to expand and document the histories of the first three generations. Since some of the fourth and most of the fifth and sixth generations were still living there seemed little need to treat them in much detail. For the most part this history ends with events or information known to us in 1970. We hope that in time others will take up the story of this Brown family and extend it both forwards and backwards in time.

Preface

The research for this history uncovered a few surprises for us personally as we found records of children who had died young and been forgotten by most family members. By far the biggest surprise was the discovery made while searching Scottish census records that William Brown, his wife Isabella, and their first four children were all born in Ireland.

Our branch of the family had always believed they were from Scotland and we had taken great pride in our Scottish heritage. When we reported this remarkable discovery to one of the older members of the family, she informed us that she had known that all along, having learned it from her father who was one of the Scottish born grandsons of William Brown, but that she hadn't told us because we were having so much fun being Scottish!

The evidence in the Scottish records is quite clear that William Brown lived in County Down in Northern Ireland. However, as will be seen from the Historical Background which follows, that does not mean that they were Irish. In fact, there is every reason to suppose that their ancestry, if traced back from that point, would lead back to Scotland. We have not undertaken research in the Ulster records which might confirm that expectation, but must leave that study to others.

In this history a seperate account is given of each person born with the surname "Brown," whether male or female, provided they lived to adulthood and there was significant information available about them. Thus the allied families into which the Brown daughters married are covered for one generation in addition to all the Brown sons. These family articles are arranged in alphabetical order according to the given name(s) of the "Brown" head of the household. Where there are articles about two or more people with the same given name(s), they are arranged in chronological order. A chart has also been included which shows the descendants of William and Isabella Brown, and identifies those who are the subjects of separate articles in this history.

References to sources of data are indicated in the early generations by abbreviations in parentheses placed at the appropriate places in the text. A key to the abbreviations used is given at the end of this section.

A great many people have contributed to the preparation of this genealogy - too many to enumerate. However, we do want to especially thank Rev. Barry Whenal and Professor Kimber G. Wheelock for their kind permission to draw on material they have compiled on the Whenal and Wheelock families, respectively.

ABBREVIATIONS USED IN THE GENEALOGIES

B - Birth record
C - Cemetery inscriptions
CWP - Civil War pension file
D - Death record
DD - Deed
DIR - Town or city directory
DV - Divorce record
ENL - *Exeter News-Letter*, Exeter, N.H.
ETR - *Exeter, N.H. Town Reports*
FR - Family record in possession of person named
HF - *History of Hampton Falls, N.H.*, Warren Brown, 1900
HRC - *History of Rockingham County, N.H.*, Charles A. Hazlett, 1914
KGW - Kimber G. Wheelock's genealogical notes
M - Marriage record
N - Naturalization records
O - Obituaries
P - Probate records
PL - Passenger lists
PR - Parish register
SC - Scottish census
USC - United States census

HISTORICAL BACKGROUND

In as much as this history records the migration of the Brown family from Ireland to Scotland, and finally to America, a brief description of the historical forces that probably moved them, and of the environments in which they lived seems an appropriate place to begin.

So far as we have learned their journey on this earth began in County Down in Northern Ireland, then called Ulster, about 1820. That area is today the scene of conflict and strife, and it seems, it has ever been so. For our purpose we will begin about the year 1607 with the flight of the Earls and the beginning of Ulster Plantation.

ULSTER PLANTATION

In the sixteenth century there had been more or less continual conflict between the Gaelic Irish and the English who were attempting to subjugate them. In 1607 the Earls of Tyrone and Tyrconnell along with nearly 100 other northern chiefs fled Ireland forever. The English took the opportunity to confiscate four million acres of their lands comprising the counties of Donegal, Derry (then called Colerine), Tyrone, Fermanagh, Cavan, and Armagh. Subsequently they annexed the counties of Antrim, Down, and Monaghan.

The formation of Ulster Plantation was finalized in 1609 when, during the reign of James I, these lands were divided among undertakers, servitors, and natives. The undertakers were mainly Englishman and were obliged to take an oath acknowledging the English supremacy in order to get their grants. They were only permitted to lease their lands to English or Scottish tenants. The servitors were mainly Scots. They were free to

1

rent to the Irish natives, but if they did so their rents to the Crown were increased. Native Irish grantees, of whom there apparently were few, were obliged to pay double the quitrents paid by the English undertakers, but were spared the necessity of taking the oath of supremacy.

The obvious objective of the English in Ulster was to drive the native Irish from the soil, and in this they succeeded admirably. Many of the natives fled to the hills where they subsisted under the most miserable conditions. Those that remained in the fertile valleys were little more than slaves. Sir John Davies in his contemporary account of the subjugation of the Irish wrote *"The multitude having been brayed as it were in a mortar with sword, pestilence and famine, althogether became admirers of the Crown of England"* (MacManus, p. 406). The latter was the wildest of wishful thinking, however, and conflict continued, as it has, indeed, right to the present time.

It was in this manner that a great many Scots as well as some English came to settle in the northern parts of Ireland. The conditions of their settlement obliged them never to alien their lands to the Irish, to adopt Irish custom, nor to intermarry with them. To refer to the Scots who settled in Ulster as Scotch-Irish is a misnomer. They retained their Scottish culture and heritage and were Irish only in a geographical sense.

Describing the character of the settlers one Stewart, son of a Presbyterian minister who was one of the planters, wrote *"From Scotland came many, and from England not a few, yet all of them generally the scum of both nations, who from debt, or breaking, or fleeing justice, or seeking shelter, came hither hoping to be without fear of man's justice"* (MacManus, p. 407). Those words may seem a bit harsh, but the immigrants to Australia, Canada and the United States have been similarly described on occasion. It is clear that people who are secure in their financial, political, and religious lives do not immigrate. To paraphrase the inscription on the Statue of Liberty, it is the tired, poor, huddled masses yearning to breathe free, the homeless, tempest-tossed, wretched refuse of one nation which flees to another. In all probability poverty was the motivating force which induced William Brown's ancestors to remove from Scotland to Ulster.

The history of the Irish and the Scotch-Irish following the settlement of Ulster Plantation is not a happy one; conflicts and rebellions repeatedly arose. Our purpose is not to recount the entire history, but rather to set the tone. This cannot be done better perhaps than to present the eye witness account of Benjamin Franklin as preserved in a letter to Dr. Joshua Babcock, postmaster of Westerly, Rhode Island. The letter was composed in London on January 13, 1772 while Franklin was there serving the Colonies.

Historical Background

I have lately made a Tour thro' Ireland and Scotland. In those Countries a small Part of the Society are Landlords, great Noblemen, and Gentlemen, extreamly opulent, living in the highest Affluence and Magnificence: The Bulk of the People Tenants, extreamly poor, living in the most sordid Wretchedness, in dirty Hovels of Mud and Straw, and cloathed only in Rags.

I thought often of the Happiness of New England, where every Man is a Freeholder, has a Vote in publick Affairs, lives in a tidy, warm House, has plenty of good Food and Fewel, with whole cloaths from Head to Foot, the Manfacture perhaps of his own Family. Long may they continue in this Situation! But if they should ever envy the Trade of these Countries, I can put them in a Way to obtain a Share of it. Let them with three fourths of the People of Ireland live the Year round on Potatoes and Buttermilk, without Shirts, then may their Merchants export Beef, Butter, and Linen. Let them, with the Generality of the Common People of Scotland, go Barefoot, then may they make large Exports in Shoes and Stockings: And if they will be content to wear Rags, like the Spinners and Weavers of England, they may make Cloths and Stuffs for all Parts of the World.

Farther, if my Caountrymen should ever wish for the honour of having among them a gentry enormously wealthy, let them sell their Farms & pay rack'd Rents; the Scale of the Landlords will rise as that of the Tenants is depress'd, who will soon become poor, tattered, dirty, and adject in Spirit. Had I never been in the American Colonies, but was to form my Judgement of Civil Society by what I have lately seen, I should never advise a Nation of Savages to admit of Civilization: For I assure you, that, in the Possession & Enjoyment of the various Comforts of Life, compar'd to these People every Indian is a Gentleman: And the Effects of this kind of Civil Society seems only to be, the depressing Multitudes below the Savage State that a few may be rais'd above it. (Fleming, Vol. 2, p. 235)

That grim picture had probably not changed greatly by 1819 when William Brown was born. But there was worse yet to come.

THE GREAT FAMINE

The potato had become the staple food of the masses in Ireland just as rice was dominant in the Orient. In 1845 an unknown blight appeared which worsened in 1846 and 1847, and

3

destroyed substantially the entire crop in 1848. That brought incredible hardships upon the people. There was widespread starvation followed by pestilence and disease. The population of Ireland dropped from about eight million to six million between the years of 1845 and 1851. Of that two million decrease about half died of starvation or disease while about a million fled the island for all corners of the earth. Of the million who fled a great many perished enroute to a new land or died in quarantine camps once they had arrived.

The suffering of the ordinary people was almost indescribable. In the *"Last Conquest of Ireland"* John Mitchel gives the following account of what he saw on a journey across what had been the fertile center of the island:

> *We saw sights that will never wholly leave the eyes that beheld them, cowering wretches almost naked in the savage weather, prowling in turnip fields, and endeavouring to grub up roots which had been left, but running to hide as the mail coach rolled by: groups and families, sitting or wandering on the highroad, with failing steps, and dim, patient eyes, gazing hopelessly into infinite darkness and despair; parties of tall, brawny men once the flower of Meath and Galway, stalking by with a fierce but vacant scowl: as if they realized that all this ought not to be, but knew not whom to blame, saw none whom they could rend in their wrath. Sometimes, I could see, in front of the cottages, little children leaning against a fence when the sun shone out - for they could not stand - their limbs fleshless, their bodies half-naked, their faces bloated yet wrinkled, and of a pale greenish hue - children who would never, it was too plain, grow up to be men and women.* (MacManus, p. 607)

During this dreadful period the English who governed the island did little to aid the Irish. Indeed many of their acts seem positively designed to worsen the lot of the masses, and a strong case can be made that they were anxious to see the native Irish die or leave. Some foreign governments, including the United States, sent aid, but the magnitude of the problem was so great that it had no great impact on the desperate plight of the people. The Quakers, the Society of Friends, was one of the few groups on the scene sincerely attempting to relieve the suffering. One of their agents gave the following report of what must have been a typical rural scene:

> *One poor woman whose cabin I had visited said, "There will be nothing for us but to lie down and die". I tried to give her hope in English aid. But alas! her*

prophecy has been too true. Out of a population of two hundred and forty I found thirteen already dead from want. The survivors were like walking skeletons - the men gaunt and haggard, stamped with the livid marks of hunger, the children crying with pain - the women in some cabins too weak to stand. All the sheep were gone - all the cows - all the poultry killed - only one pig left - the very dogs which had barked at me before, had disappeared. No potatoes - no oats. (MacManus, p. 607)

It was from that desperate scene that William Brown fled with his young family from the land of their nativity to the land, no doubt, of their ancestors, the Galloway district of Scotland.

GALLOWAY

The general geographical and historical position of Galloway is described as follows:

It must be remembered that the geographical position of Galloway, round the corner from the main north-south line and bounded by hills to the north and east, has been responsible for many peculiarities in the way in which it has developed. It remained fiercely independent when the rest of Scotland was united; the influence of England predominated at many stages of its history; its proximity to Ireland has led to a continous flow of Celtic immigrants for several thousand years; and, despite its central position in the British Isles, Galloway has remained almost completely unaffected by the industrialization of the past two centuries. It has always been essentially a rural and somewhat isolated agricultural community. (Robertson, p. 10)

One of the authors, (LCT), had the good fortune to visit the Galloway district in 1970, and to travel through Wigtonshire and see the lands where the Brown families lived and worked. We can vouch for the fact that the area is still an isolated rural agricultural community.

In traveling through Glasserton parish where the Browns were primarily located, we were amazed to see how little it had changed in the hundred years since they left there for America. Aside from electric lights and a very few automobiles there was little there that was "new". The farms on which the Brown families labored - *Stellock, Cairndoon, Carleton, Knock,* etc. are still there, still being worked, and indeed still bear the same names. Perhaps the principal change has been the emigration of

5

many of the native people, the population now being about half what it was about 1850 when the Brown family arrived there.

Galloway had always been an agricultural area with particular emphasis on raising livestock - goats, sheep and cattle - and the grasses and grains with which to feed them. The century between 1750 and 1850 which preceded the arrival of the Browns had seen great progress made in agricultural pursuits. Much waste land was brought under cultivation by draining bogs and wet areas. Some descriptions of that activity will be found at the back of this volume in the Scottish Gazetteer. It is quite possible that William Brown was himself engaged in the late stages of that improvement.

In addition, the belted Galloway cattle had been developed which commanded a higher price at the market than the best English grown beef. They are still raised there, and ironically, have in recent years been imported to the United States and are now being raised in New Hampshire but a few miles from where the Brown families first settled a hundred years ago!

The century before the Browns arrived in Galloway was also a period of industrial growth there, principally in the form of cottage industries. Many of the cottar's wives were engaged in spinning linen and woolen thread which was used in the mills in Dumfries as well as locally for the manufacture of their own clothing. A fine damask cloth was made in a factory in the village of Sorbie, and some of the cottar's wives were expert lace-makers. So far as we know the Brown families had little connection with these manufacturing activities being employed exclusively on the land. But in the 1851 census Mary Drysdale, the mother of Joseph Drysdale who married Mary Ann Brown, is listed as being employed with embroidery.

Robertson describes the living conditons of the native Gallovidians of 1850 as being much superior to that of the masses of people in the industrial cities. They were decently fed and clothed. Their diet consisted largely of oatmeal porridge or oatcakes, but was supplemented liberally with local dairy products, milk, butter and cheese with occasional mutton or beef. But he goes on to say:

> *The only people who did not enjoy such good living conditions were the Irish who crossed over into Galloway in their thousands throughout the nineteenth century. Some settled down as farm servants, but the majority were largely itinerant, seeking what seasonal work might be available and living in considerable poverty when unemployed. After the 1841 census a Wigtownshire minister estimated that one person in every five in his parish was Irish, or born of Irish parents....* (Robertson, p. 204)

6

Historical Background

We know for a fact that the Browns were farm servants and laborers. Being born in Ireland, or born of Irish born parents, even though their heritage was probably Scottish, no doubt places them within Robertson's definition of being "Irish". Thus we must expect that their living conditions were poor and their circumstances desperate. Indeed, some members of the family who were born in Scotland have recounted how they lived in a cottage with a hard-packed dirt floor and went barefoot the year round. We can therefore surmise with reasonable certainty that the motivating force which drove parts of three generations of the Brown family to emigrate to America was predominately economic.

While we have not been able to describe the environments in which the Browns lived in Ireland and Scotland with absolute certainty, we hope that this historical synopsis will provide a useful backdrop to the genealogical articles which follow.

BIBLIOGRAPHY

Encyclopaedia Britannica, Chicago, 1962, Vol. 12, article on Ireland.

The Story of the Irish Race, Seumas MacManus, 4th Rev. Ed., 1944, reprinted, New York, 1973.

The Story of Galloway, John F. Robertson, Castle-Douglas, Scotland 1963.

The Founding Fathers, Benjamin Franklin, A Biography in His Own Words, Thomas Fleming, Ed., New York, 1972.

MAPS

There are at least two excellent maps of the area which show the topographical features, roads, railroads, streams, towns, villages, and even the large farms where the Brown families lived:

Galloway 37, published by John Bartholomew & Son, Ltd., Duncan St., Edinburgh 9, Scotland, covers all of Galloway at a half-inch to the mile scale which includes details down to the large farms.

Kirkcudbright 80, published H. M. Stationary Office, First Avenue House, 49 High Holborn, W.C. 1, England, covers the portion of Galloway where the Brown families lived at a one-inch to the mile scale which provides even more detail.

THE BROWN FAMILIES

The following chapter contains a genealogical article about every descendant of William and Isabella (Kennedy) Brown who was born with the surname BROWN, and about whom we have sufficient information to justify a separate entry. The articles are arranged in alphabetical order by given name. The names of children who are the subjects of separate articles are shown in all capital letters, while the names of children who are not carried forward are not capitalized.

If you know the name of your BROWN ancestor, just look for them in the alphabetical sequence; you will then be able to move up or down the family tree from that point. If you do not know the name of your BROWN ancestor, then you will first need to use the master chart at the back of the volume to find where you connect into the BROWN family tree. The master chart shows all the known descendants of William and Isabella (Kennedy) Brown, regardless of their surname.

THE BROWN FAMILIES

ADDISON ORLAND BROWN was born at Bridgeport, Conn. on 14 March 1933, son of Nile Holmes and Emily Louise (DeLong) Brown. He served in the U.S. Army 1950-1952. Later he belonged to Co. A of the 118th Combat Engineers in Pawtucket, R.I. On 23 September 1955 he married Eva L. (Beland) Batista at Seekonk, Mass. She had three children, Paul, Kenneth and Geraldine by her previous marriage. Mr. Brown is a painting contractor in business with his step-sons. The family resided in Pawtucket, R.I. about 1970.

#+#+#+#+#+#+#+#+#+#+#+#+#+#+#

ALEXANDER S. BROWN was born on the farm called *Carleton* in Glasserton Parish, Wigtonshire, Scotland on 24 April 1857, son of Benjamin B. and Elizabeth (Thompson) Brown (B). He died at Exeter, N.H. on 31 May 1908 (D). On 25 Dec 1880 he married Henrietta M. B. Chapman at Stratham, N.H. (M). She was born in Stratham, N.H. on 22 July 1861, daughter of Edward and Abigail (Jewell) Chapman (O). After the death of Alexander S. Brown, Henrietta married George Vear. She died in Exeter, N.H. on 14 April 1966 aged 104 (O).

In 1861 Alexander S. Brown was living as a child with his parents on the farm called *Knock* in Glasserton Parish, Scotland (SC). A decade later at age 14 he was living on the same farm, where he was employed part time as a farm laborer (SC). He came to the United States with his parents on the steamship *Olympus*, arriving in Boston, Mass. on 18 April 1872 after a passage from Liverpool, England (PL). The middle initial "S" does not appear in any of these early records. According to tradition he used the nickname "Sandy" which may account for his use of that initial in later life. On 15 Oct 1878 he applied to the Supreme Court of New Hampshire to become a United States

citizen (N). Three witnesses, Orin Sanborn, John S. Tuck, and
Charles M. Bean, testified among other things that he had been a
resident of Brentwood, N.H. for more than a year (N). He was
naturalized on the following October 29th (N).

According to tradition, he worked as a young man on a
Jewell farm in Stratham, N.H. His whereabouts have not been
found in the 1880 census, but his bride-to-be was then living at
home with her parents in Stratham as shown by the following
enumeration (USC):

```
Edward B Chapman    head   66   farmer          b . N.H.
Abigail A.    "      wife   51   housekeeper        "
Asa C.        "      son    39   farm lab.          "
DeWitt C.     "      son    27      "               "
Henrietta M.B."      dau    18   at home            "
```

Later that year, on Christmas day, Alexander and Henrietta
were married in a service conducted by George W. Thompson,
Congregational minister of Stratham (M).   Tradition indicates
that Henrietta's full name was Henrietta Maria Baker Jones
Chapman, the three middle names being given her at birth in
memory of a child lost by a close friend of Henrietta's mother.
Only the middle initials M. B. have been found on records.

On 18 Feb 1885 Alexander S. Brown of Stratham and his wife
Henrietta M. Brown obtained a mortgage on a 2 acre parcel of
land in Stratham from Wm. Junkins of Greenland for $425.00
(DD). This tract apparently had a house on it, it *being the homestead formerly occupied by Charles Kelly, late of Stratham, deceased* (DD). That mortgage was discharged 22 Aug 1888 (DD).
The following September 29th Alexander and Henrietta, still
residents of Stratham, took mortgages on two parcels of land in
that town from Sarah Norton, also of Stratham (DD).   The first
tract of six acres was bounded on the north by the highway from
Exeter, N.H. to Portsmouth, N.H., and on the other three sides
by land of Samuel C. Dixon (DD).   The second tract contained
fourteen acres and was on the north side of the highway mentioned (DD). It was bounded by the land of Wm. Robie and the
heirs of John T. Smith (DD). No doubt they were involved in
other real estate transactions as well.

It is probable that Alexander farmed some of this land.   In
1880 when he married he described himself as a farmer (M), and
according to tradition he worked on a farm at Odiorne's Point at
Rye Beach, N.H. His obituary indicates that he was a carpenter,
but had also worked as a farmer (O). In 1900 when his daughter
Dora married, the marriage record indicates that Alexander and
Henrietta were residing in Rye, N.H. where he was a caretaker
(M). His death record describes him as a farmer (D).

The Brown Families

On 19 May 1908 Alexander S. Brown wrote this will (P):

I, Alexander S. Brown, being of sound mind, so declare this to be my last will and testament viz:-

First, To my daughter, Dora E. French, I bequeath the sum of one dollar.

Second, To my wife, Henrietta M. Brown, I bequeath all the remaining property of which I may die possessed and I hereby appoint her to be Executrix of this my last will and testament and request that she be not required to give bond.

In witness whereof I have hereunto set my hand and seal this 19th day of May, A. D., 1908.

Signed: A. S. B. Brown

Witnesses: Herbert C. Day, Emma L. Sanborn, and Emma Bartlett.

Following his death this obituary appeared in the *Exeter News-Letter* of 5 June 1908:

Mr. Alexander S. Brown died Monday morning in his fifty-second year, at his home on Linden Street, a portion of the William Burlingame house. For about a year he has been ill with a stomach trouble, and for two weeks under the care of a trained nurse. Throughout his illness, which he bore with patience and fortitude, his wife was constant in her ministrations. Mr. Brown was born in Scotland, April 24, 1857, the oldest of ten children of Benjamin B. and Elizabeth Brown, and his is the first death in the large family. When fourteen years old he came to this country and has since lived in Brentwood, where his father was long an officer of the county farm; in Stratham, Exeter and Merrimac, Mass., whence he returned to Exeter ten months ago. He was by trade a carpenter, and has also been a farmer. He was a past master of Winnicut lodge, A.F.& A.M., at Greenland, and upon its ceasing to exist he became a member of St. John's lodge at Portsmouth.

Mr. Brown leaves besides his wife, a daughter, Mrs. Charles French, of Exeter, his parents, six brothers and three sisters; Mrs. Isabelle K. Bartlett, Mrs. Elizabeth C. Purington, and Mrs. Jennie W. Morrison.

The funeral was held at the home at 2 P.M. Wednesday, and was conducted by Rev. George H. Driver of the First Church. The Beethoven quartet sang three selections and Mr. Frank H. Lamson a tenor solo. St. John's Lodge, A. F. & A. M., of Portsmouth performed its committal ritual, assisted by members of Star in the East lodge. The bearers were the six brothers, William of Auburn, Maine;

13

The Brown Families

Robert and John D. of Amesbury; Andrew of Brentwood; Benjamin and George B. of Exeter.

The widowed Henrietta removed to Rollingsford, N.H., near Dover, where she kept house for a Mr. Hayes. She was living in Dover in 1916 (DIR). Later she moved to Westfield, N.Y. where she met George Vear whom she married as her second husband. He owned vineyards in Westfield, N.Y., near Buffalo, and was well-to-do. They lived there until his death. She then returned to Exeter, N.H. where she remained the rest of her long life. On 22 July 1964 a special celebration was held at her home on Ash St., in Exeter to mark her 103rd birthday. She received greetings from President Lyndon B. Johnson, Senators Norris Cotton and Thomas McIntyre, Congressman Louis Wyman, Governor John King and former Governor Wesley Powell, as well as many personal friends.

It had been thought that Henrietta died intestate, but about three years later as her grandson, Clarence B. Hoitt, was preparing to vacate the house on Ash Street the following will was found. Since there were no known assets the will was placed on file so that it could be probated at a later date should any be found (P):

Be it known that I, Henrietta M. Vear, widow, of Exeter, Rockingham County, New Hampshire, so make this my last will and testament hereby revoking all former wills by me made.

First: I appoint George E. Wright of Exeter, Executor of this will and do request that he be excused from giving any bond for the faithful discharge of his duties (except such bond as the law requires).

Second: I have not forgotten the offspring of my late Grandson Harry Hoitt, deceased, but for good reasons I do not care to leave any property to them. They are my great grand children: - Scott Hoitt, Dale Hoitt, Linda Hoitt, and Frank Hoitt.

Third: All the rest, residue and remainder of my estate, real and personal and mixed, wherever situated, I give and devise to my grandson, Clarence B. Hoitt (of Exeter). If he survives me and not otherwise. I most earnestly and sincerely request that he husband and conserve this property out of REGARD to me and my memory and that he use it only for the necessaries of life and not for luxuries.

If said Clarence B. Hoitt does NOT survive me, but leaves a widow, I give one-third of this remainder to said widow and the other two-thirds to my nieces: Caroline Stearns, Cora Cooper, Bertha Russell, Maude Tytus, Mollie

The Brown Families

Trask, and Helen Tuck, or to such of said nieces as may survive me. If said Clarence does NOT survive me and leaves no widow, then I give all said remainder to said nieces, above named or such of said nieces as may survive me.

In witness whereof, I have hereunto set my hand and seal at Exeter N.H., this 23rd day of September, A.D. 1953.

Signed: Henrietta M. Vear

Witnesses: Mary B. Mathes, Mary W. Fisher, and Perley Gardner.

Alexander S. Brown and Henrietta M. Vear are buried in the Linden Street Cemetery in Exeter where the inscriptions read:

Alexander S. Brown   1857-1908
Henrietta B. Vear   1861-1966

BROWN child:

DORA ELIZABETH - b. Exeter, N.H. (M) on 30 Jan 1882.

#+#+#+#+#+#+#+#+#+#+#+#+#+#

ALICE LENA BROWN was born at Amesbury, Mass., on 26 May 1912, the daughter of John William and Abbie Edith (Anderson) Brown. She died young as indicated by the following three items from the *Amesbury Daily News*. The first two are from the issue of 9 Jan 1928, and the third is from the issue of January 11th:

DEATH: BROWN, in Amesbury, Mass., 8 Jan 1928. Miss Alice L. Brown, age 15 years, 9 months, and 12 days. Funeral services from the home 5 Myrtle Street, Tuesday afternoon at 2 o'clock.

Sorrow has come to the home of Mr. and Mrs. John W. Brown through the death of one of their child, Alice L., which occurred at the family home early last evening following an illness of a few weeks' duration. She was born in Amesbury March 26, 1912, and entered High School as a freshman last fall. She was an attendant of the Market Street Baptist Church and a member of the Bible School, also of the Camp Fire Girls, Camp Cheskechamay. Alice was a bright, lovable girl and had a great many friends. Besides her parents, a younger sister and brother survive her. The sympathy of the Community is extended to the bereaved family.

*Funeral services will be held from the family home at
2 o'clock, Tuesday afternoon. Relatives and friends are
invited.*

*The last rites for Miss Alice L. Brown were held from
the family home 5 Myrtle Street yesterday at 2 o'clock.*

*There was a very large attendance of relatives,
friends, classmates, and members of the Camp Fire Girls.
There was also an unusual number of beautiful floral tributes.*

*Rev. Ralph A. Stone was officiating clergyman; he
brought a very helpful and comforting message.*

*Morris Currier, George Temple, Walter Diamondstone,
Woodbury Currier, Richard Briggs, and William Broe of
the High School served as bearers.*

*The interment was in the family lot in Mt. Prospect
Cemetery where a committal service was held. The undertakers were Pillsbury and Gale in charge of arrangements.*

#+#+#+#+#+#+#+#+#+#+#+#+#

ANDREW C. BROWN was born in Glasserton Parish,
Wigtonshire, Scotland (SC) on 16 June 1859 (C), son of William
and Isabella (Kennedy) Brown (M). He died in Hampton Falls,
N.H. on 23 June 1936 (C). On 20 March 1886 he married Rose
Matilda, daughter of Samuel and Martha Glover, at Hampton
Falls (M). She was born in Nottingham, N.H. (M) on 20 March
1867 (C), and died, probably in Portsmouth, N.H., on 19 April
1951 (C).

Andrew C. Brown came to America on the steamship *Palmyra* with his parents in 1870 (PL). In 1870 he resided at home
with his parents in Hampton Falls and was attending school
(USC). In 1880 he was still living there, but was employed as a
shoemaker (USC). He was also following that trade in 1886 when
he married (M).

Andrew C. and Rose M. Brown always resided with his
parents on Lafayette Road in Hampton Falls. They celebrated
their fiftieth wedding anniversary as described in the following
notice from the Hampton Union of March 1936:

*HAMPTON FALLS, March 22 - Mr. and Mrs. Andrew
C. Brown, highly respected residents of Hampton Falls,
yesterday observed their golden wedding anniversary.
They were guests last evening at the home of Mr. and Mrs.
Edwin L. Janvrin.*

*Mr. Brown was born in Scotland June 16, 1858, and
came to Hampton Falls with his parents in 1870. He was
engaged in farming here and the past 16 years has been*

Andrew C. & Rose M. (Glover) Brown

employed as a gardener by Rev. Charles L. White, a retired clergyman.

Mrs. Brown was formerly Miss Rose M. Glover. She was born March 20, 1867, in Nottingham. The couple were married here 50 years ago by Rev. Isaac Burgess of the Baptist church in the old Baptist parsonage known now as the Wellswood Inn. They have resided, since their marriage, in the same home on the Lafayette road. The couple has no children.

In 1918 Andrew C. Brown wrote the following will:

I, Andrew C. Brown of Hampton Falls, New Hampshire being of sound and disposing memory, do make this my last will and testament, hereby revoking any and all other wills, by me made at any time.

After the payment of my funeral charges and debts, I bequeath to my wife, Rose M. Brown, all of my property both real and personal, where ever found or situated.

I hereby appoint my wife, Rose M. Brown, Executrix of this my last will, and I request that she be not required to give bond.

In witness whereof I have set my hand at said Hampton Falls this 20th day of February, 1918.

Signed: Andrew C. Brown.

Witnesses: Charles N. Dodge, Frank H. Lord, and Ellen F. Lord.

This will was presented for probate on 8 Sept 1936 (P). On 26 Oct 1937 Rose M. Brown was appointed executrix and William Brown of Hampton was appointed appraiser of the estate (P). His return notes the one acre homestead, ten acres of pasture land, and one acre of marsh land (P). This William Brown is presumed to be the nephew of Andrew who served as undertaker (P).

The following obituary appeared in the *Exeter News- Letter* of 3 July 1936:

HAMPTON FALLS - Andrew Brown, who has lived in this town over 60 years coming from Scotland when a child, died suddenly at his home last Tues. The funeral was held on Thursday, with Rev. Mr. Weymouth officiating. He leaves a wife, who was Miss Rose Glover, of Nottingham. Last Year their golden wedding anniversary was celebrated. There are no children.

Mr. Edwin L. Janvrin was appointed conservator of the estate of Rose M. Brown (P). On 21 Aug 1941 he sold the ten acres of pasture land mentioned above to Andrew L. Wheelock, a nephew of Andrew C. Brown, and his wife Susan M. Wheelock of Hampton Falls (P). This was land Andrew C. Brown had acquired from his brother William H. Brown et al by deed dated 29 Oct 1892 (P). Another part of the estate was sold to David M. and Agnes Tower (P).

Andrew C. Brown and his wife are buried in Brookside Cemetery in Hampton Falls in his parents lot where the inscriptions read:

Andrew C. Brown   b. 16 June 1859   d. 23 June 1936
Rose Matilda Glover   b. 20 March 1867 d. 19 Apr 1951

#+#+#+#+#+#+#+#+#+#+#+#+#+#+#

ANDREW G. BROWN was born in Glasserton Parish, Wigtonshire, Scotland (SC) on 4 March 1866 (FR). He believed he was born in the village of Monrieth, but no record has been found. He was the son of Benjamin B. and Elizabeth (Thompson) Brown (M). He died in Northwood, N.H. on 30 June 1950 (D). On 9 June 1890 he married Nora V. Holmes at Nottingham, N.H. in a ceremony conducted by J. E. Whitmore of that town (M). Nora V. Holmes was born at Nottingham (M) on 18 March 1867, the daughter of Noah W. Holmes, a Civil War pensioner of that town, and his wife the former Lucia A. (Glover) Tuttle (CWP). Lucia A. Tuttle had been born to a Glover family, but was raised by a Tuttle family and assumed that surname prior to her marriage (CWP). Nora V. (Holmes) Brown died in Northwood, N.H. on 20 Dec 1945 (D).

As a boy Andrew G. Brown lived on the farm called *Knock* in Glasserton Parish, Scotland where his father was employed as a farm laborer (SC). Andrew G. Brown was attending school in 1871 while the family resided on *Knock* (SC). This farm is just a short distance from the village of Monrieth. The following year at age 6 he came to the United States with his parents on the steamship *Olympus* which arrived in Boston, Mass. on 18 April 1872 (PL). He has related to his daughter how his grandmother Thompson stood on the dock waving a white handkerchief as they sailed away, and how sad he felt at the thought of never seeing her again.

The family took up residence in Brentwood, N.H. shortly after arriving in America. In 1880 Andrew G. Brown was living in Brentwood with his parents and was attending school (USC). He has recounted how his father, who was a very stern man, thought nothing of having one of the boys get out of bed at night to walk two or three miles to a small general store in Epping for a cut of tobacco. Often times the store keeper would give them

Andrew G. & Nora Viva (Holmes) Brown

Clyde L. (Brown) Buzzell, Andrew G. Brown
Carla L. Burklund (child)

a piece of candy which was enough inducement to make them want to go in any weather. He has told of making this trip barefoot in winter, and how his feet would burn when he got home and into a warm bed. On dark nights he would be half scared to death and would run most of the way.

Andrew G. Brown was first boarded out as a farm hand on the Veasey Farm in Brentwood and later on the Roby Jewell Farm in Stratham, N.H. Following that he worked in the Pillsbury shoe shop in Northwood, N.H. where he met his bride-to-be, Nora V. Holmes. She was employed at the shoe shop as a forelady. It was the major industry there then employing many of the townspeople. At about that time Andrew G. Brown adopted the initial "G" which does not appear in earlier records, but does appear on his marriage record. According to tradition, he assumed the middle name Garfield because of his admiration for the twentieth American President, James A. Garfield.

Following their marriage the Browns lived briefly at Crawley's Falls in Brentwood. Then on 7 Aug 1890 Andrew G. Brown of Brentwood bought for $1500 a 30 acre homestead in Nottingham, N.H. from Lucia A. Holmes, his mother-in-law (DD). This property on the Portsmouth and Concord Turnpike, now Route 4, is located near the intersection with Garland Road. It is the same property which was purchased by John C. Holmes, the grandfather of Nora V. (Holmes) Brown, from Peletiah Jones on 1 April 1857 (DD).

Back at the turn of the century singing and playing instruments were primary forms of entertainment. Andrew and Nora Brown both had fine voices and often sung together to entertain their guests; she also played the organ. The *Exeter News-Letter* of 2 Jan 1891 has a brief account of the Christmas eve "entertainment and tree" held at Freeman's Hall near the Brown's home in Nottingham. Mention is made of how *the audience listened with much pleasure to the fine songs by Andrew Brown, and highly enjoyed the laughable comedy 'The Way They Kept a Secret'*.

Subsequently the Browns moved to Odiorne's Point at Rye, N.H. where they lived on land that later was part of a U.S. Government Military Reservation and which recently was made a State Park. They then removed to Wallis Sands, also at Rye Beach, where they lived on the Parson Farm. The farm produce was taken to market in Portsmouth. The family also took in summer boarders which was a common practice in those days. Clyde Lind (Brown) Buzzell has told how she stood and picked meat from lobsters for the guests, and did stacks of dishes when she was still so small she had to stand on a chair to reach the sink. In the following letter she describes some of the events of those years:

The Brown Families

March 3, 1969
Northwood, N.H.

Dear Laird, Marlene, and family,

Eight forty-five A.M. and snowing. It's a northeast storm and the weather reports on the radio and T.V. are that we are to get four to six inches of snow on top of the three feet we already have from the last storm of Feb. 27th. Today Apollo #9 is to be launched at eleven A.M. Weather in Florida at Cape Kennedy is said to be fine. This about takes care of the date and weather conditions.

Because of the stormy day here, it seems like a good time to relate a story which the attached picture brings to mind.

My folks were living on the "Parson" farm at Wallis Sands, at Rye, N.H. in 1902. They had moved there from a house that then was one and one-half miles farther up the coast called Odione's Point, and now owned by the U.S.Government.

The "Parson's Farm" of 320 acres was formerly a "Captain Dow" property. Captain Dow and family and two negro slaves (man and wife) are all buried in a small enclosed cemetery on a knoll on what is known as "Parson Road" on this property. A Lewis Parson, Philadelphia lawyer, bought this Dow property and this is where it got the name "Parsons". This land ran way out to the ocean, but a road now runs way 'round the ocean's edge and in to Newcastle and Portsmouth. All the field land on the ocean's edge has been built up with some very nice homes. On this land my father raised corn, potatoes, and fodder for his cattle. We always had around twenty-five cows, four horses, and two ponies.

When I was nine years old I used to drive one of the ponies named "Flossy" in to Portsmouth every Saturday with butter, eggs, chickens and vegetables for our regular customers, and when this was finished I would go to the Grocery Store and get what groceries my mother wanted and had made a list for. I went alone, and only nine years old. (What a contrast to these times and all the terrible things that happen to little girls today.) I had to drive about four miles to Portsmouth, about half of the way through real thick woods and not many houses until nearly in to Portsmouth. Today there are no woods left, all homes all the way.

My father had a pair of dappled gray work horses, "Admiral" and "Joe", both very pretty horses. "Admiral" was the gentlest one and a pretty good driving horse. My mother always claimed him as her horse. I do not know whether she paid for him or how he became her horse, but he was always HERS.

In the Summer of 1902, in August, after the haying was all done, my mother thought she would like to visit Northwood and Nottingham, her old home towns where she had many friends and relatives. It was decided to go to Northwood on a Monday morning, after my father had checked the train schedule to be sure of the exact time of the train crossing on the bridge that spanned the Piscataqua River between Portsmouth and Dover Point. (Very near where the General Sullivan Bridge is today.) The reason for not wanting to be on the bridge at a time when a train was crossing was because mother was unsure of how the horse would act, his not being accustomed to seeing steam trains, and with her, besides myself, (ten years old), were my two brothers, Nile who was eight, and Chester just a year old baby. I held that baby in my arms and on my knees from Rye to Northwood. Safely over the bridge, we poked along up through Durham and on to the Turnpike toward Nottingham. The road then was just a dirt or sand road, with plenty of dust and lots of hills which at that time were called "The Merry Hills", but of course now are all filled in and blacktop roads. This stretch of hills was a long hard pull for a horse, and the August sun was pretty hot! Our conveyance was a nice bird's eye maple Cocord Wagon - a two seater and all upholstered with dark brown leather. A real classy kind of wagon for a farmer to own! (This trip took at least six hours, and "Admiral" provided the horse power).

Upon reaching Northwood we went directly to my Uncle Forrest's home. It was a two tenement house about half a mile beyond where we now live. Some years back that house burned and a new house sits there today. (The old house was called the "Tasker House".) Uncle Forrest worked in the old shoe shop here in town as a shoe cutter.

We made many visits with my mother's relatives during the five days that we were in Northwood. One place I remember of calling at was this very house that Lester and I now own, and is our home. Little did I think then that I would some day live in it myself. I recall sitting out on the veranda while my mother visited with Arthur and Dora Holmes whose home it was then. This is the second house we have lived in since coming to Northwood, although we have owned four other properties here in town in times past.

Today would have been my father's birthday, March 4, 1866. He would be 103 years old.

21

The Brown Families

Guess this is the end of my story, but can write some others - tales about the ship wrecks that I saw while I lived at the "Parson's Farm", it you would be interested.
Love to all - Grammie Buzzell

The Parson Farm ran down to the ocean in those days and the children went there to play.   They had a Newfoundland dog, named Shep, who watched over them and kept them from wading out into the water too far by gripping their clothing in his teeth and pulling them back.   There was no road along the coast then as there is today, only a beaten path which was patrolled by a "night-watch" who carried a lantern and walked his beat throughout the night in all kinds of weather watching for ships in distress.   In severe storms the fields would be flooded, even up to the vicinity of the farm house, and would be left covered with sea foam in which the children loved to walk barefoot.   Occasionally, ships were wrecked on the shore.   On one occasion, the dog led them to the wreckage of a ship which had been carrying timber for the bridge that was then being built between Hampton Beach, N.H. and Salisbury Beach, Mass.   Andrew G. Brown and his team, Admiral and Joe, were engaged to collect the salvable timber, which was scattered along the beach, and transport it to the bridge site.   When completed that bridge became the longest wooden pile bridge in the world, but has since been replaced by a steel drawbridge.

The Browns later parted and lived most of their adult lives separated, but they never divorced.   After they separated he worked as a turnkey at the Rockingham County (N.H.) jail for eight years.   He was thus employed in 1910 when his daughter married (M).   He worked as a carpenter and was employed by the trolley line as a motorman on the run from the car barns in Atkinson, Mass. to Hampton Beach, N.H.   He built a house in Atkinson and lived there for a time.   His final employment was as a gardener and handyman for a well-to-do lady who resided at 18 Glenwood Street in Amesbury.   He had a small appartment attached to her garage.   One of the writers (LCT) spent a week of summer vacation with him there each year for two years running in the mid-1940s.   Mr. Brown remained there until he was about eighty-two when he removed to Northwood, N.H. and resided with his daughter for the last two years of his life.

Andrew G. Brown was a Mason; on 18 Jan 1897 he was raised to the degree of Master Mason in the St. Johns Lodge of Portsmouth, N.H.(FR).   An obituary from an unidentified Amesbury newspaper indicates that he had lived there for forty years, had been employed as a maintenance carpenter for a number of years in Haverhill, Hampton and Exeter, and was later employed by the Massachusetts Northeastern Street Railway lines.   It also notes that he moved to Northwood, N.H. to make his home with his daughter two years before his death, and that he was also survived by a son, Nile Brown of Attleboro, Mass., a sister, Mrs. Frank Bartlett of Brentwood, N.H., and a brother, Benjamin Brown of Bradford, Mass., and several nieces and nephews, including former Selectman Benjamin A. Brown Amesbury.

Nora V. (Holmes) Brown lived with her children in Exeter, N.H. about 1907 (DIR). First she lived on the Epping Road and was employed at the Steven Gale Shoe Factory on upper Front Street. Her daughter, Clyde, left Robinson Female Seminary and went to work at that shoe factory as a bookkeeper. Later Nora Brown operated a boarding house in Exeter at 25 Union Street. About 1914-1920 she lived in Worcester, Mass. where she was employed by the Daniel Green Slipper Factory. Later she removed to Northwood, N.H. where she was housekeeper and companion to an elderly couple, a Civil War veteran, John William Pierce Laskey and his wife, Sarah Abbie. They willed her their house and she remained there for the remainder of her life doing practical nursing and handiwork at which she was especially adept. She was a member of the First Baptist Church at East Northwood. In her will dated 11 Sept 1937 she bequeathed to her daughter, Clyde Lind (Brown) Buzzell of Northwood, N.H., and her son Nile Holmes Brown of Pawtucket, R.I. (P).

Andrew G. Brown and Nora V. (Holmes) Brown are buried in the North Side Cemetery in Nottingham, N.H. on Garland Rd. not far from where they lived as newly-weds.

BROWN children:

CLYDE LIND - b. Nottingham, N.H. on 18 Sep 1892.

NILE HOLMES - b. Odiorne's Point, Rye Beach, N.H. on 15 Oct 1894.
CHESTER JORDAN - b. on the Parson Farm, Rye, N.H. on 6 Aug 1901.

#+#+#+#+#+#+#+#+#+#+#+#+#+#+#+#

ANNE JENNIFER BROWN was born at Lewiston, Me. on 17 January 1951, the daughter of Bremner Howard and Marcia Merrow (McCarthy) Brown. She graduated from Haverhill High School in 1970. She was a Brownie, Girl Scout and a Rainbow Girl. She enjoyed piano, swimming and skiing. Miss Brown was killed in a traffic accident in 1975.

#+#+#+#+#+#+#+#+#+#+#+#+#+#+#+#

23

The Brown Families

ARLENE BARBARA BROWN was born at Attleboro, Mass. on 6 April 1955, the daughter of Nile Holmes and Lorriane (Meunier) Brown. Her interests include sewing, cooking and athletics in addition to music. During high school she spent her spare time in volunteer work assisting mentally retarded children.

#+#+#+#+#+#+#+#+#+#+#+#+#+#+#+#

BARBARA MAYNES BROWN was born at Haverhill, Mass. on 11 August 1915, the daughter of Howard G. and Jennie Mildred (Watt) Brown. She graduated from Haverhill High School in 1933. She has worked for many years as a clerk-typist in the Tax Assessor's Offices in Haverhill and Andover, Mass. On occasion she has also worked at Bradford Junior College Bookstore and Long Hill Orchards. Her interests center around art, gardening, sewing, genealogy and archaeology. She is a member of the Merrimack Valley Archaeological Society.

On 18 August 1951 she married Leonard Joseph Marble in Bradford, Mass. He was born in Haverhill, Mass. on 24 November 1918, the son of William Harry and Hannah Marie (Gill) Marble. He graduated from Haverhill High School in 1936. Mr. Mable is a commercial farmer raising tomatoes and strawberries. He formerly was in the poultry and egg business and has also worked for others in that line. He also worked for the J. P. Stevens Textile Company in the carding room before it moved south. Mr. Marble has been active in 4-H groups on the Poultry Judging Team and as a leader. He was a member of the Bradford Grange. He is interested in horse racing and ice skating.

MARBLE Children:

Thomas Howard – b. Haverhill, Mass. on 6 July 1952. He worked for Western Electric about 1970.

Janet Constance – b. Haverhill, Mass. on 11 September 1954. She worked for the Canteen Corp. at the Western Electric plant about 1970.

#+#+#+#+#+#+#+#+#+#+#+#+#+#+#+#

BEATRICE MAY BROWN was born at Exeter, N.H. on 5 June 1910, the daughter of George C. and May (Lee) Brown. She died at Portsmouth, N.H. on 25 December 1967 and is buried in the Exeter Cemetery. She married (1) Dwight Amos Standish at Exeter, N.H. on 18 February 1927 at age sixteen. He was born in Exeter in 1909, the son of Dwight C. and Mary C. (Gale) Standish. They had two children listed below, and divorced in July 1935.

Howard G. & Jennie (Watt) Brown (left)
Benjamin & Annie (Maynes) Brown (center)
Leonard J. & Barbara M. (Brown) Marble (right)

Beatrice May Brown

The Brown Families

Beatrice May Brown subsequently married (2) Mahlon A. Clough at Portsmouth, N.H. He was born in Portsmouth on 11 October 1916, the son of Mahlon L. and Pauline A. (Davidson) Clough. He died 17 December 1971 and was buried in the family lot in Central Cemetery in Rye, N.H.

STANDISH children:

Gordan Amos - b. Exeter, N.H. on 8 August 1928.

Elaine - stillborn Exeter, N.H., February 1931.

#+#+#+#+#+#+#+#+#+#+#+#+#+#

BENJAMIN BROWN was born in Glasserton Parish, Wigtonshire, Scotland (SC) on 23 Nov 1867 (FR), the son of Benjamin B. and Elizabeth (Thompson) Brown (D). He died at his home in Bradford, Mass. on 14 Feb 1954 and is buried in Elmwood Cemetery in Haverhill, Mass. (D). On 23 Nov 1889 he married Annie Maynes at Exeter, N.H.(M). She was born 4 Feb 1871 probablay in Enniskillen, County Fermanagh, Northern Ireland. She was the daughter of John and Jane (Symington) Maynes, both of Ireland, he being a farmer (M). Annie (Maynes) Brown survived her husband and died in a rest home in Haverhill, Mass. on 8 June 1959. She is also buried there in Elmwood Cemetery.

Benjamin Brown lived as an infant on the farm called *Knock* in Glasserton Parish, Wigtonshire, Scotland where his father was employed as an agricultural laborer in 1870 (SC). In 1872 he came to the United States which his parents arriving in Boston, Mass. on the steamship *Olympus* on 18 April 1872 (PL). The family subsequently took up residence in Brentwood, N.H. where Benjamin was attending school in 1880 (USC). His education terminated at about the fifth grade.

In 1889 when he married Annie Maynes at age twenty-two he was still a resident of Brentwood and was employed as a shoemaker (M). Annie Maynes was eighteen and a housekeeper residing in Exeter (M). Family sources indicate that she came to America with a sister, Elizabeth, and a cousin, Margaret (Maggie) Hunter. They arrived about 1887 and Annie found employment as a maid and cook in the home of Professor Cilley at the Phillips Exeter Academy. The marriage of Benjamin Brown and Annie Maynes was conducted by Edward Goodridge, clergyman of Exeter (M). Family sources indicate that they were married in the Episcopal Church or parsonage in Exeter.

They first lived in Fremont, N.H. where their first child was born. While they were on a shopping trip to Exeter their house in Fremont burned down. They then removed to Exeter where we find them living with their son, Howard, about 1907-8 (DIR). At that time Benjamin Brown worked in a shoe factory (DIR). He is known to have worked as foreman in the lasting room at the Gale Bros. Shoe Factory in Exeter. He also worked intermittently as a carpenter. While the family resided in Exeter three additional children were born, but all died as infants.

About 1910 the family removed to Fifth Avenue in Haverhill, Mass. where a building boom was taking place and where Benjamin Brown was employed as a carpenter. He subsequently built a home on Hawthorne Street in nearby Bradford, Mass. where the family resided for a time. About 1913 he built a house at 303 Salem Street in Bradford where he lived until his death in 1954 (D).

Annie (Maynes) Brown enjoyed handiwork such as crocheting, knitting, braiding rugs, etc. For a time while they lived in Bradford she worked as a fancy stitcher in shoeshops in Haverhill. She also had a "green thumb" and raised vegetables and flowers.

Annie was five feet two inches tall with blue eyes, while Benjamin was tall, a Brown trait, at six feet one inches; he also had blue eyes. Benjamin Brown was an avid horseman and kept horses when they lived in Exeter and again in Bradford. He was especially interested in harness racing and had several trotting horses which his son Howard, and grandson Bremner, raced at fairs in Maine, New Hampshire and Massachusetts. Benjamin Brown occasionally played a harmonica and he loved to sing, another trait which he shared with many other members of the family.

BROWN children:

HOWARD GEORGE - b. Fremont, N.H. on 28 Nov 1890 (O).

Male - b. Exeter, N.H. on 7 Aug 1892 (ETR); died about age one year.
Female - b. Exeter, N.H. on 19 May 1893; died the following day (ETR).
Male - b. Exeter, N.H. on 11 Aug 1894 (ETR); died about age one year.

#+#+#+#+#+#+#+#+#+#+#+#+#+#+#

BENJAMIN ALEXANDER BROWN was born in Amesbury, Mass. on 11 January 1909, the son of John D. and Elizabeth (Elliott) Brown. He married (1) Kathryn H. Gorman in Elkton, Md. on 2 January 1934. She died without issue at their home in Albuquerque, N.M. on 12 February 1971. He married (2) Mrs. Evelyn Louise Barrett who died 18 January 1975. She had several children from her previous marriage.

Benjamin & Annie (Maynes) Brown (left)
Bremner H. Brown & Barbara M. Brown (center)
Howard G. Brown (right)

Benjamin A. Brown & Isabel W. Brown

The Brown Families

Mr. Brown operated a grocery store in Amesbury for many years, and served as a Selectman, 1945-1947. He entered the credit field as a collector in 1934 and worked his way up to the position of District Manager from which he retired in September of 1964. After that he was Executive Director of Consumer Credit Counseling service of Albuquerque Inc., a non-profit debt counseling service for the State of New Mexico, from which he retired on 30 December 1977.

#+#+#+#+#+#+#+#+#+#+#+#+#+#+#

BENJAMIN B. BROWN was born in Ballyholde, Ireland on 3 May 1837, son of William and Isabella (Kennedy) Brown (D). He died in Amesbury, Mass. on 10 Aug 1918 (D). On 11 Dec 1856, after banns according to the Church of Scotland, he was married to Elizabeth Thompson, daughter of Alexander and Elizabeth (Campbell) Thompson (M). She was born in Glasserton Parish, Wigtonshire, Scotland on 17 Oct 1835 (PR), and died at Amesbury, Mass. on 5 Sept 1919 (D).

Benjamin B. Brown moved from Ireland to Scotland with his parents sometime between the years 1846-1849 as can be deduced from the birth places of his younger brothers and sisters in the Scottish census records. In 1851 he was living with his parents on the farm called *Stellock* in Glasserton Parish, Wigtonshire, Scotland where he was an unmarried farm laborer (SC). When he married in 1856 he was a farm servant on a farm called *Culkae* in Sorbie Parish, and note is made of the fact that he had previously been at *Cairndoon* in Glasserton Parish (M). His bride, Elizabeth Thompson, was described as a spinster domestic servant (M). The marriage took place on the farm called *Carleton* where Elizabeth resided, and was conducted by Arch. Stewart, minister of Glasserton (M).

Elizabeth (Thompson) Brown was the youngest of six children of Alexander and Elizabeth (Campbell) Thompson found recorded in the Glasserton Parish records (PR). In the 1841 census the family resided on the farm called *Carleton* where they were enumerated as follows (SC):

```
Alexander Thompson  38 ag. lab.  b. Wigtonshire
Elizabeth      "    45    -              "
Jess           "    14    -              "
Elizabeth      "     6    -              "
```

Also living at *Carleton* in a separate household was John Thompson, age 15, and Margaret Thompson, age 17, both born Wigtonshire (SC), whom we presume to also be children of Alexander Thompson. In 1851 the family was still residing at *Carleton* (SC):

27

The Brown Families

```
Alexander Thompson head 50 farm lab.      b. Sorbie,
                                             Wigtonshire
Elizabeth       "    wife 58       -        b. Glasserton,
                                             Wigtonshire
Jess            "    dau  23       -        b.     "
Elizabeth       "    dau  17 outdoor lab.  b.     "
infant(name n.k.)g.son  8 days             b.     "
```

When his first child was born in 1857 Benjamin B. Brown was still a farm servant at *Culkae* and Elizabeth was at *Carleton* (B), apparently living with her parents who were still there in the 1861 census (SC). In 1861 we find Benjamin B. Brown and family on the neighboring farm called *Knock* where he was a ploughman (SC):

```
Benjamin Brown  head  22 ploughman  b. Ireland
Elizabeth    "  wife  25       -    b. Glasserton
Alexander    "  son    3       -    b.     "
William      "  son    2       -    b. Whithorn
Robert       "  son    9 mo.   -    b. Glasserton
```

Ten years later in 1871 after his parents, brothers, and sisters had all emigrated to the United States, Benjamin B. Brown and his family were still residing at *Knock* in Glasserton Parish (SC):

```
Benjamin Brown  head  32 ag. lab.   b. Ireland
Elizabeth    "  wife  35 farm lab.  b. Glasserton
Alexander    "  son   14    "            "
William      "  son   12    "       b. Whithorn
Robert       "  son   10    "       b. Glasserton
John         "  son    9 scholar         "
Isabella     "  dau    7    "            "
Andrew       "  son    5    "            "
Benjamin     "  son    3    -            "
Elizabeth    "  dau    2    -       b. Kirkinner
```

Although Benjamin B. Brown lived principally in Glasserton Parish, it appears from the births of his children William and Elizabeth that he resided in the nearby parishes of Whithorn and Kirkinner in the years 1859 and 1869, respectively (SC).

The family emigrated to the United States in 1872 after Benjamin B. Brown's brother arranged for him to become agricultural foreman at the Rockingham County Farm in Brentwood, N.H. They arrived in Boston, Mass. on 18 April 1872 on the steamship *Olympus* (PL). They came in steerage as did the rest of the family (PL). Their names appear on the passenger list as follows (PL):

28

Benjamin B. & Elizabeth (Thompson) Brown
(standing in an onion patch)

The Family of Benjamin B. & Elizabeth (Thompson) Brown

Benjamin B., Jennie W., Benjamin, Elizabeth C., Andrew G., Elizabeth
George C., John D., Robert L., William, Alexander S., Isabel K.

The Brown Families

Benjamin Brown	40	laborer
Elizabeth	"	38	–
Alexander	"	14	laborer
William	"	11	"
Robert	"	9	–
John	"	7	–
Isabella	"	5	–
Andrew	"	3	–
Benjamin	"	1	–
Elizabeth	"	1	–

When the family first arrived in this country they lived in a small house in Brentwood, N.H. near the County Farm. On 14 March 1878 Benjamin B. Brown bought two tracts of land from Hannah Sinclair and Mary E. Weeks, both of Concord, N.H., for $744.00 (DD). One tract contained about 60 acres situated in Brentwood and Fremont; the other contained about 1 acre situated in Brentwood (DD). Subsequently he acquired other property in the vicinity of the Brentwood Baptist Church including a house in which they lived during the remainder of their residence in Brentwood.

Benjamin B. Brown declared his intention of becoming a U.S. citizen on 18 April 1878 and was naturalized at the Supreme Court in Exeter, N.H. on 27 April 1880 (N). In that year the family was enumerated in the census as follows in Brentwood (USC):

Benjamin B. Brown	head	43	foreman C.F.	b.	Scot.
Elizabeth	"	wife	42	housekeeper		"
William	"	son	21	teamster C.F.		"
Isabella	"	dau	16	school		"
Andrew	"	son	14	"		"
Bennie	"	son	12	"		"
Lizzie	"	dau	11	"		"
Jennie	"	dau	8	"	b.	N.H.
George	"	son	5	–		"

Another son, John D., age 17, was a farm laborer boarding on the neighboring farm of William W. Veazy in Brentwood (USC).

In January of 1910, while residents of Brentwood, Benjamin B. Brown and wife Elizabeth sold a 2 1/2 acre parcel of land there to Joseph Proulx for $1.00 (DD). Shortly thereafter they removed to Amesbury, Mass. where they lived with their son John D. Brown. On 8 July 1913 while residents of Amesbury, Mass., Benjamin B. and Elizabeth Brown sold four tracts of land in Brentwood and Fremont, N.H., including those originally purchased in 1878, to George W. Bryant and G. Stillman Bryant, both of Brentwood for *$1.00 and other considerations* (DD).

29

The Brown Families

During their residence in Brentwood the Brown family posed for a group photograph which was taken at the Tilton studio on Linden Street in Exeter. It was probably about that same time that they had the following family record printed (FR):

PARENTS

Benjamin B. Brown	Born	May 3, 1837
Elizabeth Brown	"	Oct 17, 1835

CHILDREN

Alexander S. Brown	Born	Apr 24, 1857
William Brown	"	Jan 30, 1859
Robert Brown	"	Jul 6, 1861
John D. Brown	"	Jan 19, 1862
Isabelle K. Brown	"	Apr 8, 1864
Andrew G. Brown	"	Mar 4, 1866
Benjamin Brown	"	Nov 23, 1867
Elizabeth C. Brown	"	Jul 23, 1869
Jennie W. Brown	"	Jun 6, 1872
George C. Brown	"	Aug 18, 1875

Several copies of the group photograph and family record are still extant.

The following obituary for Benjamin B. Brown is taken from an unidentified newspaper clipping. It is presumed to have appeared in an Amesbury paper since a similar, but not identical, article appears in the *Exeter News-Letter*. The list of floral tributes provides a small census of the family in 1918.

> *Benjamin B. Brown, a former resident of Brentwood, died in Amesbury, Mass., Saturday, August 10, at the home of his son John D., where he and his wife had for eight years made their home.*
>
> *Mr. Brown lived to be 81 years old. He was born in Maureeth, Scotland, and in 1872 went to Brentwood to take the position of foreman at the Rockingham County Farm, which he held for 30 years. He was a farmer of prominence, due to his successful methods in that work. It was said of him, by those qualified to know, that "He was the best farmer in Rockingham County." His rare ability at farming; his knowledge of making his own farming tools and the models for the same helped to gain for him that enviable record. He was called "Uncle Ben" at the farm and outside of that institution the name has always clung to greetings extended him.*

30

The Brown Families

He was a member of the Brentwood Baptist Church in which he took a great interest. Eight years ago Mr. and Mrs. Brown took a letter from that church to become members of the Market Street Church in Amesbury.

Mr. Brown was a man of high standing, kindhearted, generous toward helping others and was highly respected by all that knew him.

A wife and eight children survive. They are William, of Auburn, Me.; John D. and Andrew G., of Amesbury; Benjamin, of Haverhill; George C., of Exeter; Mrs. Frank Bartlett, of Brentwood; Mrs. Elizabeth Purinton and Mrs. Jennie Morrison, of Exeter. Three brothers and three sisters also survive. There are 21 grandchildren and 14 great grandchildren.

Funeral services were held at the home of his son, John D., Monday, August 12, at one o'clock. There were many relatives, friends and neighbors present, who went to honor the memory of a long, well spent life. Rev. S. James Cann, his pastor, conducted the services and Mrs. John Jordan sang two selections, "Beautiful Isle of Somewhere" and "Does Jesus Care." The bearers were his brothers, John, Andrew, and William Brown, and Joseph Drysdale. The body was conveyed by auto hearse to Brentwood for interment in the family plot. A committal service was held at the grave.

The floral tributes were very beautiful and profuse, viz.: Pillow, "Husband," Mrs. Benjamin B. Brown; standing lyre, "Father," Mr. and Mrs. William Brown, Mr. and Mrs. John D. Brown, Mr. and Mrs. Benjamin Brown, Andrew Brown, George Brown, Mrs. Frank Bartlett, Mrs. Elizabeth Purinton, Mrs. Jennie Morrison; pillow, "Brother," Mr. and Mrs. John Brown, Mr. and Mrs. Andrew Brown, Mr. and Mrs. William Brown; basket, "Grandpa," grandchildren; spray of white roses, Mr. and Mrs. Joseph Drysdale; spray of pink gladioli and white asters, great grandchildren; spray roses, Mrs. Robert Brown; spray purple and pink gladioli, Mr. and Mrs. S.A. Jenness; spray roses, Mr. and Mrs. George Dearborn, Mr. and Mrs. Carroll Osgood; floral wreath, Mrs. Etta Brown, Mr. and Mrs. Charles French, Clarence Hoyt, Harry Hoyt; spray of purple and white chrysanthemums, Mr. and Mrs. John Downer and family; spray red gladioli, James E. Watkins; spray purple and white asters, Mr. and Mrs. John W. Lamprey; spray pink and white asters, Mr. and Mrs. Joseph Hume; garden bouquet, Mr. and Mrs. William Graves; garden bouquet, Mr. and Mrs. W.P. Hodge and family; garden bouquet, Mrs. F.A. Hodge; ; spray gladioli, Mr. James H. Curtis and family; spray pink and white chrysanthemums, Mrs. Joseph Yell and family.

The Brown Families

The death of Elizabeth (Thompson) Brown was reported in the *Exeter News-Letter* as follows:

BRENTWOOD, September 17 - Elizabeth Brown, widow of the late Benjamin B. Brown, passed away at the home of her son, John D. Brown, September 5th. Mrs. Brown was born in Glasserton, Scotland, October 17, 1835, and married there, coming to America in 1872 and settling in Brentwood, where they lived until ten years ago, when they went to Amesbury to make their home with their son, John D. In her earlier years, although she had a large family to care for, there being ten children, she found time to take part in all the activities of the Brentwood Baptist Church, of which she was a beloved member. On her removal to Amesbury she transferred her membership to the Market Street Baptist Church. A fine Christian woman has been called home. Eight children survive her: William, of Auburn, Me.; Mrs. Frank H. Bartlett, of Brentwood; Benjamin, Jr., of Bradford, Mass.; Mrs. Elizabeth C. Purinton, Mrs. Oscar Morrison and George C. Brown, of Exeter; John D. and Andrew G., of Amesbury. Alexander S. and Robert passed away several years ago. The names great grandmother, grandmother and mother are dearly cherished. Rev. S. James Cann, her pastor, and Rev. Bernard G. Christopher, a former pastor of her home church in Brentwood, conducted the service. Two beautiful hymns, "Saved by Grace" and "Lead Kindly Light," were rendered. These hymns fitingly reflected the spirit and life of the deceased. The remains were brought by auto hearse to Brentwood for interment in the family lot where a committal service was held. Beautiful floral tributes silently spoke of the love and esteem in which she was held. Quietly she was laid to rest beside her beloved companion who preceded her a year ago.

Benjamin B. Brown and his wife are buried in a family plot in Brentwood, N.H. where the inscriptions read:

```
Benjamin B. Brown    1837-1918
Elizabeth Brown      1835-1919
```

BROWN children:

ALEXANDER S. - b. on the farm called *Carleton*, Glasserton Parish, Wigtonshire, Scotland, on 24 April 1857 (B).
WILLIAM - b. on the farm called *Morrach*, Whithorn Parish, Wigtonshire, Scotland, on 30 Jan 1859 (B).

ROBERT L. - b. Glasserton Parish, Wigtonshire, Scotland (SC) on 6 July 1861 (FR).

JOHN D. - b. on the farm called *Knock*, Glasserton Parish, Wigtonshire, Scotland (SC) on 19 Jan 1862 (B).

ISABEL K. - b. on the farm *Garrarie*, Glasserton Parish, Wigtonshire, Scotland on 8 April 1864 (B).

ANDREW G. - b. Glasserton Parish, Scotland (SC) on 4 March 1866 (FR).

BENJAMIN - b. Glasserton Parish, Wigtonshire, Scotland (SC) on 23 Nov 1867 (FR).

ELIZABETH C. - b. Kirkinner Parish, Wigtonshire, Scotland (SC) on 23 July 1869 (FR).

JENNIE W. - b. Brentwood, N.H. (M-William H. Burke) on 6 June 1872 (FR).

GEORGE C. - b. Brentwood, N.H. (M) on 18 Aug 1875 (FR).

#+#+#+#+#+#+#+#+#+#+#+#+#+#+#+#

BERNICE ARLENE BROWN was born at Worcester, Mass. on 20 April 1921, the daughter of Nile Holmes and Emily Louise (DeLong) Brown. As a young woman she sang in a trio with her sisters, Marjorie and Vivian. They were known as "The Brown Sisters", and appeared on a local radio station. She married (1) Kenneth I. Estabrook on 13 May 1939 at Bridgeport, Conn. He was born in Massachusetts on 30 May 1926, the son of Irving Estabrook. They had a daughter. She married (2) Robert A. Meunier in Central Falls, R.I. on 8 Nov 1945. He was born in Pawtucket, R.I. and served in the U.S. Navy for many years. He died in England in January 1970. No issue. She married (3) Donald Peter Adams at Pawtucket, R.I. on 27 June 1959. He was born there on 19 Dec 1919, the son of William H. and Dora Emma (LaSalle) Adams. Mr. Adams is a steeplejack. He has four children by a former wife, Lillian: Donald William, Robert Roland, Joyce Marie and Linda Lee. Mr. and Mrs. Adams resided in Central Falls, R.I. about 1970.

ESTABROOK child:

Vivian Jean - b. Bridgeport, Conn. on 19 Sept 1944.

#+#+#+#+#+#+#+#+#+#+#+#+#+#+#+#

BEVERLY JUNE BROWN was born at Newburyport, Mass. on 28 September 1931, the daughter of Clyde Wallace and Ruth Amelia (Brown) Brown. She married Ralph Bilodeau at Manchester, N.H. on 11 October 1952. He was born there on 4 November 1928. He was foreman of the paint finishing department of Work Place Systems about 1970. She was a supervisor at Edison

The Brown Families

Electronics in Manchester, N.H. and lived in Merrimack, N.H about 1981. No children.

#+#+#+#+#+#+#+#+#+#+#+#+#+#+#+#

BETTY JANE BROWN was born at Exeter, N.H. on 2 March 1924, the daughter of Robert O. and Helen Mae (Kimball) Brown. She married Earl Blatchford at Hampton, N.H. on 23 Aug 1947. He served in the U.S. Coast Guard during WWII, 1942-1946, and is a printer by trade. Mrs. Blatchford is a high school teacher.

BLATCHFORD children:

Janet Elaine - b. Exeter, N.H. on 28 Oct 1949.

Joyce Ann - b. Exeter, N.H. on 15 Sept 1951.

#+#+#+#+#+#+#+#+#+#+#+#+#+#+#+#

BREMNER HOWARD BROWN was born in Bradford, Mass. on 4 May 1922, the son of Howard G. and Jennie Mildred (Watt) Brown. His unusual given name was the maiden name of his great grandmother Watt who came from Scotland. He graduated from Haverhill High School in 1940 receiving the Wright Prize in chemistry. He then entered Tufts College from which he graduated *Magna Cum Laude* in 1944 with a B.S. degree in Chemical Engineering.

While in college Mr. Brown was a member of the Student Council, was Vice President of his class, and was a member of *Deta Tau Delta* fraternity. He received the Travelli Scholarship, was a member of the Sword and Shield honor society, was treasurer of the Ivy Society, another honor society, and belonged to the engineering honor society *Tau Beta Pi*.

Mr. Brown is a sports enthusiast. He played baseball in high school and college, being shortstop on the Tufts team. He also enjoys bowling and tennis.

Mr. Brown entered the Navy in 1944 and served as a communications officer for seventeen months at Pearl Harbor. He was discharged in 1946 as a Lt. (jg). He shared his father's love of harness racing and spent the next four years driving "Hiworthy" at fairs, especially throughout Maine. He was Presiding Judge on the State of Maine Racing Circuit 1948-1951 while he was employed as a superintendent at the Thoms and King Lumber Mill in South Paris, Maine. In 1951 he moved to the Engineering Department of the Western Electric Company bringing his family first to Haverhill and then to Bradford where they now reside. Mr. Brown has been a member of the Boy Scouts, DeMolay and Masons.

34

Mr. Brown married Marcia Merrow McCarthy at Waterville, Me. on 22 May 1948. She was born in Winslow, Me. on 21 July 1922, the daughter of Maurice Franklin and Frances (Johnson) McCarthy. She graduated from the Winslow Maine High School in 1939 where she played trumpet in the school band. In 1943 she graduated from the University of Maine with a B.A. degree in Economics. Prior to her marriage she was a feature writer for the Guy Gannett Publishing Co. of Portland, Me., specializing in harness racing news. From 1962 until the present she has taught elementary school. In 1968 she received an M.A. degree in Education from Salem State Teacher's College. Mrs. Brown enjoys antique collecting, skiing and swimming. She is a member of the Haverhill College Club and the Haverhill Day Nursery Association.

BROWN children:

ANNE JENNIFER - b. Lewiston, Me. on 17 January 1951.

MARCIA FRANCES - b. Haverhill, Mass. on 28 August 1953.
NANCY MERROW - b. Haverhill, Mass. on 22 Jan 1957.

#+#+#+#+#+#+#+#+#+#+#+#+#+#+#

CHESTER JORDAN BROWN was born on the Parson Farm, Rye, N.H. on 6 Aug 1901, the son of Andrew G. and Nora Viva (Holmes) Brown. The following clipping from an unidentified newspaper reports his untimely demise:

At the North Nottingham Church, on Tuesday afternoon, February 1, Rev. G. W. Collins, of Northwood Ridge, conducted a funeral service over the remains of Chester Jordon Brown, who, on the night of Friday, January 28, was accidentally asphyxiated by gas escaping from a jet piece in a bedroom of his home in Worcester, Mass. Burial was in the North Side cemetery.

The deceased was a son of Andrew G. and Norah (Holmes) Brown, formerly of Nottingham. His age was 19 years, 5 months, and 22 days. He was a young man of sterling qualities, and an apt scholar. He was a student, in his first year, of the Worcester Polytechnic Institute. Besides his parents and maternal grandmother, Mrs. Lucia A. Ham, Mr. Brown has left one sister, Mrs. Lester Buzzell, of Worcester,and one brother, Nile H. Brown, of Bridgeport, Conn. Many feel sad at the sudden termination of his bright and promising life.

The Brown Families

CLARENCE WARREN BROWN was born in Greenland, N.H. on 19 March 1883, the son of Robert L. and Ida A. (Winn) Brown. He died at Frisbie Memorial Hospital in Rochester, N.H. on 25 June 1969 at age 86 (O). He married (1) Thannie Wales Gleason at Reading, Mass. on 20 Oct 1909. She was born in Cambridge, Mass. on 7 July 1882, the daughter of Walter P. and Emma Gleason. They divorced on 28 Dec 1928. Thannie Wales Brown was an assistant cook in the cafeteria of the Portsmouth Jr. High School for many years. She died in Brentwood, N.H. on 25 March 1964, and is buried in South Cemetery in Portsmouth where the inscription reads:

Thannie W. Brown   b. 7 July 1882   d. 25 March 1964

Clarence Warren Brown was employed at various times as a conductor, fireman, and engineer by the Boston and Maine Railroad, and also worked as a carpenter. Family sources indicate that he was the youngest engineer on the B & M at one time. On 4 July 1943 he married (2) Mrs. Susie E. Tebbetts who was born in Rochester, N.H. on 23 Dec 1894. She had been married once previously and had sons Donald, Bernard, and Foster Tebbetts. At the time of his death in 1969, Clarence Warren Brown had been a resident of the Rochester area for ten years. He belonged to the Unity Masonic Lodge in Union, N.H., the Miltonia Lodge of Odd Fellows in Milton Mills, and the Brentwood Baptist Church (O). He is buried in Rochester Cemetery (O). His widow resided in Rochester in 1970.

BROWN children:

MARION BEATRICE - b. Marblehead, Mass. on 29 July 1910.
NORMAN ROBERT - b. North Conway, N.H. on 5 July 1912.

RICHARD CLARENCE - b. Portsmouth, N.H. on 15 Jan 1916.

#+#+#+#+#+#+#+#+#+#+#+#+#+#

CLYDE LIND BROWN was born in Nottingham, N.H. on 18 Sept 1892, the daughter of Andrew G. and Nora V. (Holmes) Brown. She died at Tri-County Osteopathic Hospital in Kittery, Me., on 10 Jan 1970 after a brief illness and is buried in the family plot in the cemetery at Lee Hill, N.H. On 3 Jan 1910 she was married to Charles Lester Buzzell at Exeter, N.H. in a ceremony conducted by Rev. E. A. Wellman of the First Baptist Church there.

The Brown Families

Charles Lester Buzzell was born at Newfields, N.H. on 14 Aug 1890, the son of Arthur Chester and Maybelle Florence (Burgess) Buzzell. Mr. Buzzell had a noteworthy natural talent for mechanical arts which stood him in good stead throughout his life. When his father died at an early age, he left school to help support the family. He was apprenticed to a jeweler, W. E. Farnham of Exeter, N.H., from whom he learned the watchmaker's trade. He followed that trade at least part-time for most of his life; during his middle years he operated the Turnpike Watch Shop in Northwood, N.H. in addition to his regular employment at the Portsmouth Naval Shipyard.

When over seventy years of age he climbed up to the steeple of the First Baptist Church in East Northwood, N.H. where he spent many days of difficult labor remaking and repairing the three-faced clock which had been inoperative for many years. His home resounded with the ticking and striking of many varieties of clocks over the years. The peak of his barn at his final home in Northwood, N.H. boasted a large round clock which he designed and installed so that all passersby might check the time.

As a young man, Mr. Buzzell worked as a chauffeur for several wealthy families along Boston's North Shore when automobiles first came into vogue. He drove Locomobiles and other early models, and has recounted chauffeuring for J. P. Morgan, the financier, on one occasion when he was a house guest.

Later Mr. Buzzell worked as a machinist for the Waldron Worcester Wrench Co. in Worcester, Mass. In September 1920, because of the ill health of one of his children, he moved to the country taking his family to Northwood, N.H. There he was the machinist in the C. K. Fox shoe factory for many years. Although this factory was small, it turned out special orders of shoes for such celebrities as Clara Bow, Theda Bara, and Jean Harlow. During WWII Mr. Buzzell was employed at the Portsmouth Naval Shipyard where he was a "lay-out" man setting up work for the machinists. Later he was employed as a machinist at the Bourque Bros. Shoe Factory in Raymond, N.H. For many years Mr. Buzzell also operated a real estate office in Northwood.

Mr. Buzzell joined the Masons while living in Worcester and later transferred his membership to Morrison Lodge #90 in Northwood. He became a fifty-year mason in November of 1970. He was also a member of the Odd Fellows and the Jr. O.U.A.M.

Clyde Lind Brown resided as a child on the Parson's Farm at Wallis Sands in East Rye, N.H. There she attended the Octagonal school. This building was constructed of sea stones in 1896 and is now a private residence. During summers her parents took in vacation guests, as was then the fashion, and she

37

frequently was occupied with kitchen chores such as washing dishes and picking out lobster meat. One of her favorite chores was taking the farm produce to market in Portsmouth. This she did by herself driving her pony "Flossie" and a cart filled with produce to a market where she also filled her mother's grocery list for the return trip home; these chores she tended to as a young child.

It was while the family resided in Rye that Clyde Lind Brown began attending the Robinson Female Seminary in Exeter. She, along with a cousin, Pearl Bartlett, boarded with their aunt, Mrs. George C. Brown, on the Epping Road in Exeter while school was in session. They shared an unfinished upper room and became life-long friends. While staying at Aunt May's, she returned home weekends on the electric cars.

During this period her parents separated causing her to leave school and seek employment. She obtained a position as payroll bookkeeper at the Gale Bros. Shoe Shop in Exeter where her mother also was employed. Following her marriage Mrs. Buzzell was occasionally employed in shoe factories in the various cities and towns where the family resided.

Mrs. Buzzell's skills and accomplishments in the domestic arts equalled those of her husband in the mechanic arts. She created many prize-winning hooked pictures and rugs, and enjoyed many forms of hand work. She also excelled in culinary art. She had a great sense of home and family, and took great pleasure in preserving heirlooms, pictures, and family records. Her life-long love for family history is the seed from which the present work has grown; we all owe her a great debt.

Mr. and Mrs. Buzzell both inherited musical talents. She played the piano and he the violin. Following the custom of the times, when guests called they would entertain them musically, not infrequently with their whole family participating. Music and song was a common part of their way of life. When they first settled in Northwood in 1920, they furnished the music for the weekly country dances, playing waltzes, fox trots, and two-steps, as well as jigs and reels for the old fashioned dances such as Portland Fancy, Virginia Reels, and various Quadrilles.

Mr. Buzzell was a particularly versatile musician and could play many band instruments besides violin, banjo, and drums. For twelve years he was director of the Northwood-Epsom Band, playing for various town affairs as well as in the surrounding area. For several seasons he directed the Sunday evening concerts held in the Band Stand at the summer resort of Alton Bay, N.H. on the edge of Lake Winnepasaukee. His eldest daughter played the drums in his band.

At about the age of seventy, Mr. Buzzell took up oil painting for the first time, and created many fine original paintings, which together with specimens of his wife's fine handiwork, now grace the homes of their many descendants and friends. Mr. Buzzell died 31 July 1974 and is buried beside his wife in Lee Hill Cemetery.

BUZZELL children:

Meryl Leola – b. Exeter, N.H. on 27 Mar 1910.

Wilma Lois – b. Brookline, Mass. on 3 Jan 1913.

Ruth – b. Worcester, Mass. on 6 Nov 1914; d. young.

Ruth Irma – b. Worcester, Mass. on 13 Jan 1919.

#+#+#+#+#+#+#+#+#+#+#+#+#+#+#

CLYDE WALLACE BROWN was born in Hampton, N.H. on 26 August 1899, the son of William and Cora Eva (Blake) Brown. He married Ruth Brown, daughter of Rufus Smith and Maude Amelia (Little) Brown of Salisbury, Mass. on 15 September 1929 at Salisbury, Mass. She was born there on 25 February 1906. Mr. Brown died 2 November 1980 while living at Leisure Village in Manchester, N.H., and was buried in High Street Cemetery in Hampton.

Mr. Brown was a salesman for the American Mat Co. He was a member of the Candia Kinnicum Fish and Game Club, and had been its treasurer for many years. He was also a member of the United Commercial Travelers and a past member of the Auburn Lions Club.

He was survived by his wife, Ruth; a son, William of Auburn; two daughters, Mrs. Beverly Bilodeau and Mrs. Judith Prentiss, both of Merrimack; four grandchildren; and several nieces and nephews.

BROWN children:

BEVERLY JUNE – b. Newburyport, Mass. on 28 September 1931.
JUDITH LEE – b. Newburyport, Mass. on 20 July 1933.

WILLIAM SMITH – b. Manchester, N.H. on 12 August 1940.

#+#+#+#+#+#+#+#+#+#+#+#+#+#+#

CORA HAZEL BROWN was born at Hampton, N.H. on 3 May 1901, the daughter of William and Cora E. (Blake) Brown. On 13 April 1926 she married Norman Marston Coffin. He was born in Hampton on 30 Sept 1898, the son of Morrill and Georgia Coffin.

The Brown Families

The following account of their wedding appeared in the *Exeter News-letter* of 9 April 1926:

> *The large social event of the week was the marriage of Miss Cora H. Brown, daughter of Mr. and Mrs. William Brown, and Mr. Norman Coffin, son of Georgia and the late Morrill Coffin, on Saturday afternoon in the home of the bride. The ceremony was witnessed only by the immediate friends of the contracting parties and was performed by Rev. John Cummings with the double ring ceremony. The bride came into the march of honor, her father giving her in marriage, and was met there by the groom and his best man, Clyde Brown, brother of the bride. The maid of honor was Miss Josephine Moulton, of North Hampton, a niece of the groom. Miss Moulton looked sweet gowned in white and carried sweet peas. Later the ushers, Russell Moulton, brother-in-law of the groom, and Robert Brown, brother of the bride, were kept busy escorting the large number of guests present at the reception to offer congratulations to the bride and groom.*
>
> *The bride has always been one of Hampton's most popular young ladies as she always had a pleasant smile and cheery word for young and old. The groom always popular, has made himself doubly so since his management of the A & P store by his graciousness.*
>
> *The bride was gowned in white silk crepe and carried bridal roses. All extend hearty congratulations to Mr. and Mrs. Coffin. After a bridal trip to New York and other places of interest in a new Lincoln Car, the happy couple will reside in one of the Mason tenements.*
>
> *The Wedding March was played by Mrs. Elliot. The presents were not only numerous, but beautiful and useful.*

Mr. Coffin died in 1969, and was buried in High Street Cemetery in Hampton. At his funeral the honorary bearers were Roscoe Palmer and Charles Greenman; the bearers were Judge John W. Perkins, Russell Hammond, Norman Merrill, Gerard Richard, Malcolm Hamilton, and John Callahan; and the ushers were Samuel Towle, Carl Bragg, and Clifford Bean. Attending in a body were selectmen, directors of the Hampton Cooperative Bank, members of the Odd Fellows, employees of the Callahan Oil Co. and Hampton Police Department.

Mrs. Coffin died 22 Jan 1979 at her home at 56 Dearborn Avenue in Hampton. She had been town tax collector for many years, retiring in 1971, and a clerk at the Hampton Post Office. She was also employed at the Bean Insurance Agency, Hampton. She was was a member of the Hampton Congregational Church and its Women's Guild; the past president of the Hampton

Monday Club, the Hampton Historical Society, and the Professional Women's Club, of Portsmouth. She was also an advisor for the recreation department in Hampton. She was survived by a brother, Clyde W. Brown, of Raymond, and several nieces and nephews. Mr. and Mrs. Coffin had no children.

#+#+#+#+#+#+#+#+#+#+#+#+#+#+#

DAVID NILE BROWN was born at Central Falls, R.I. on 28 Feb 1950, the son of Nile Holmes and Lorraine (Meunier) Brown. He attended California State College in Fullerton, Calif. where he studied communications with a view to a teaching career or working in the media. He was voted "Student of the Year" from among 410 young men for which he received a large trophy. He has won scholarships for wrestling, public speaking, and a special teacher's scholarship which was voted him by the teachers of Anaheim.

#+#+#+#+#+#+#+#+#+#+#+#+#+#+#

DORA ELIZABETH BROWN was born in Exeter, N.H. (M) on 30 Jan 1882. She was the daughter of Alexander S. and Henrietta M. (Chapman) Brown. She died on 15 June 1953 (ETR). She married (1) Clarence Harrison Hoitt; (2) Charles W. French.

On 25 June 1900 Dora Elizabeth Brown married Clarence Harrrison Hoitt at Portsmouth, N.H. in a ceremony conducted by Myron Tyler, clergyman, of Portsmouth (M). She was residing with her parents in Rye, N.H. at the time (M).

Clarence Harrison Hoitt was born in Dover, N.H. on 29 June 1880, the son of Harrison O. and Anniebelle (Jackson) Hoitt (O). He followed the printers trade as a young man, as had his father (M). Following their marriage the couple resided in Portsmouth, N.H. where their two children were born (B). Clarence Harrison Hoitt was also a talented pianist and was so employed at times, but his primary occupation was as a printer. He served overseas in WWI, and was a member of the Frank E. Booma American Legion Post, and the Emerson Hovey Post, VFW.. The couple divorced. He remarried and had additional children. He removed to Chicago, Ill. about 1940 and died there on 4 July 1957 while living at 751 West 87th Street. Survivors included his wife, Mrs. Alice Hoitt, three sons, Clarence of Exeter, Ernest of Seattle, Wash., and Edward Hoitt; a sister, Mrs. Pearl H. Shaw of Portsmouth; two brothers, Ernest R. Hoitt of Portsmouth and Raymond J. Hoitt of Quincy, Mass.; four grandchildren, a great-grandchild and several nieces and nephews. He was buried in Portsmouth, N.H.

Dora Elizabeth (Brown) Hoitt married as her second husband Charles W. French of Brentwood, N.H., about whom we have

41

learned very little. They resided on Court St. in Exeter, N.H. where he died on 22 May 1945 (P). She died suddenly in 1953 while visiting one afternoon with a relative, Mrs. Pearl Block, in Brentwood, N.H.

Mrs. French was a member of Christ Church (Episcopal) of Exeter; Orient Chapter Order of Eastern Star of Exeter, and the White Shrine of Portsmouth; Gilman Grange, and the Thursday Circle of the Congregational Church. She was survived by a son, Clarence Brown Hoitt of Exeter, and her mother, Mrs. Henritta Vear of Exeter, and three grandchildren (of her late son, Harry H. Hoitt).

She was buried in the family lot in the Exeter Cemetery where the following pertinent inscriptions are to be found on a large Brown monument:

```
Charles W. French   b. 1882   d. 1945
Dora E. French      b. 1882   d. 1953
```

HOITT children:

Clarence Brown – b. Portsmouth, N.H. on 27 Dec 1901 (B).

Harrison Heffenger – b. Portsmouth, N.H. on 7 march 1903 (B).

#+#+#+#+#+#+#+#+#+#+#+#+#+#

ELIZABETH C. BROWN was born 23 July 1869 (FR) in Kirkinner Parish, Wigtonshire, Scotland (SC). She was the daughter of Benjamin B. and Elizabeth (Thompson) Brown (M). She died in Merrimac, Mass, on 19 Aug 1942 and is buried in Prospect Cemetery in Epping, N.H. (D). She married (1) Charles A. Osgood; (2) Ira C. Purinton; (3) Wilbur A. Shipley.

Elizabeth C. Brown was living with her parents on the farm called *Knock* in Glasserton parish, Wigtonshire, Scotland in 1871 at age 2 (SC). The following year she came to America on the steamship *Olympus* which arrived in Boston, Mass. on 18 April 1872 (PL). In 1880 she was residing at home with the family in Brentwood, N.H. where she was attending school (USC). On 30 Nov 1889 she married Charles A. Osgood at Exeter, N.H. in a ceremony conducted by Rev. Swift Byington of Exeter (M).

Charles A. Osgood was born in Fremont, N.H. about 1868, the son of Bruce D. and Mary A. (Purington) Osgood (M). He was a shoemaker residing in Fremont, N.H. in 1889 when he married Elizabeth C. Brown (M). They were divorced on 8 Oct 1898 (DV) after having one child. Elizabeth C. Osgood was made sole guardian of their son Caroll W. Osgood on that same date (P). We know nothing further of Charles A. Osgood.

Elizabeth C. Brown

A few years later on 30 May 1903, Elizabeth C. Osgood married Ira C. Purinton at Epping, N.H. in a ceremony performed by Rev. T.G. Tangdale of Epping (M). Ira C. Purinton was the son of Hendrick G. Purinton, farmer of Epping, N.H., and his wife the former Sarah E. Eaton (M). He was a shoe operator in 1903 when they married and his bride was employed as a shoe stitcher (M). He was a resident of Epping, and she of Fremont, at that time (M). Ira C. Purinton was born at Epping (M) on 9 Nov 1867 (C). He died on 8 Feb 1906 (C).

Following the death of her second husband, Elizabeth C. Purinton lived in Exeter, N.H. where she worked at the Gale Bros. Shoe Shop. About 1916 she was boarding at 11 Harvard St. in Exeter with her son Carroll W. Osgood and his first wife, Bessie (DIR). On 25 April 1920 she married as her third husband Wilbur A. Shipley (ETR). It was his second marriage (ETR). The following notice of the wedding appeared in the *Exeter News-Letter* of 30 April 1920:

> *Mr. Wilbur A. Shipley, an Exeter merchant, and Mrs. Elizabeth Campbell Purinton were married Sunday afternoon by the Rev. Dr. James W. Bixler, at the bride's home, 26 Auburn Street, (Exeter) where they will reside.*

Wilbur A. Shipley operated a novelty shop at 65 Water St. in Exeter where Isabel (Brown) Bartlett was manager (ENL-8 July 1921). He also had a shop at Hampton Beach, N.H. He died in Exeter late in 1932 as noted in the following obituary from the *Exeter News-Letter* of 9 Dec 1932:

> *Coming with surprising suddenness early Thursday morning was the death of Wilbur A. Shipley at his home at 117 Front Street. Mr. Shipley was a man of sterling qualities, is remembered by many as the propritor, for many years, of a novelty store at Hampton Beach and later at Exeter.*
>
> *Mr. Shipley came to Exeter from Lowell, Mass., about 13 years ago, opening a store in what is now a part of the Exeter and Hampton Electric light offices. He retired from active business about four years ago.*
>
> *Mr. Shipley was born in Londonberry, Aug 16, 1862, the son of Daniel T. and Ellen F. (Abbott) Shipley. He is survived by his wife in Exeter, and two half sisters, Mrs. Nellie A. Morris, of Nashua, and Mrs. Ian B. Wilson, of Boston.*

Subsequently Elizabeth C. Shipley removed to Merrimac, Mass. where she kept house for her son. She lived there about ten years prior to her death at age 73 in 1942 (D). On her death record and in one newspaper account of one of her marriages her middle name is given as Campbell while family sources have said it was Cecil. We think the former is more likely correct since her maternal grandmother's maiden name was Elizabeth Campbell.

Cemetery inscriptions in Prospect Cemetery in Epping, N.H. read as follows:

```
Ira Purinton   b.  9 Nov 1867   d.  8 Feb 1906
Ethel (no dates)
Carroll W. Osgood   b.  1890   d.  1945
```

OSGOOD child:

Carroll W. - b. Brentwood, N.H. (ETR) 25 Nov 1893 (FR).

PURINTON child:

Ethel - died as an infant.

#+#+#+#+#+#+#+#+#+#+#+#+#+#

ELLA MARGARET BROWN was born in Brentwood, N.H. on 28 Aug 1893, the daughter of John D. and Elizabeth (Elliott) Brown. She died in Amesbury, Mass. on 11 July 1948. On 15 June 1913 she married Thomas Bush White in Amesbury. He was born there on 25 June 1890, the son of James Goodrich and Mary (Osgood) White. Thomas Bush White was an electrician and a fireman. He died intestate on 3 Aug 1944 while a resident of Amesbury (P). The Widow, Ella M. White, was appointed administratix of his estate in which the three children listed below are mentioned (P). The following notices of Mr. White's-death appeared in the *Amesbury Daily News* of 3 and 7 Aug 1944, respectively:

DEATHS: WHITE, in Amesbury August 3rd. Thomas B. White, 84 Congress Street, Captain of Engine 3 of the Amesbury Fire Department, aged 54 years, 1 month, 8 days. Funeral from the Pillsbury and Gale Funeral Home Sunday afternoon at 2:30. Visiting hours Saturday evening from 7 to 9.

Funeral services for Thomas B. White, former Captain of Engine 3, Amesbury Fire Department, who died at his home, 88 Congress Street, last Thursday, were held yesterday afternoon at 2:30 from the Pillsbury and Gale Funeral Home. Rev Sven Laurin, pastor of the Methodist Church officiated.

The Brown Families

Members of the local fire department, attired in dress uniform, attended the services in a body and provided an escort for the funeral cortege from the funeral home to Union Cemetery. The spacious funeral home was crowded with many friends and associates in addition to the fire department. A large delegation from the Henschel Corporation, headed by C. R. Hensel, President of the corporation, was present. Mr. White was lately employed by the firm.

This great company of sorrowing friends together with the profusion of floral tokens which completely covered Engine 2, used as a floral car, gave mute testimony to the esteem with which the deceased was held by all who knew him.

The bearers were Fire Chief George A. MacDougall, Deputy Chief Louis J. Bartley, James Scott O'Neill, acting Captain of Engine 3, Lt. Howard G. Bagley, Lt. C. H. Gage, Lt. James W. MacLean, Sr., David L. Currier, and Hector Provencher.

Interment took place in Union Cemetery with Rev. Mr. Sven Laurin performing the committal service.

Ella Margaret (Brown) White died in Amesbury on 11 July 1948 and is buried there in Union Cemetery, as described in the following clippings from the *Amesbury Daily News* issues of 12 and 14 July 1948, respectively:

DEATHS: WHITE. Suddenly in Worcester, July 11, 1948, Ella M. White, widow of Thomas B. White, formerly of this town, aged 54 years, 10 months, and 13 days. Funeral services from the Pillsbury and Gale Funeral Home, Tuesday afternoon at 2 o'clock. Burial in Union Cemetery. Visiting hours Monday evening from 7 to 9 P.M.

Funeral services for Mrs. Ella M. White, widow of Thomas B. White, of 70 Congress Street, who died suddenly on Sunday in Worcester while visiting her sister, were held yesterday afternoon from the Pillsbury and Gale Funeral Home. Rev. Sven A. Laurin, pastor of the First Methodist Church, was the officiating clergyman.

The service was attended by a large number of relatives and friends, and there were many beautiful flowers.

The bearers were Fire Chief George A. MacDougall and Lt. Charles H. Gage of the local fire department, and Hartwell Reid and James Reid. Interment took place in Union Cemetery.

45

WHITE children:

Mabel Frances - b. Amesbury, Mass. on 30 Jan 1914.

James Goodrich - b. Amesbury, Mass. on 2 May 1916.

Thomas Bush - b. Amesbury, Mass. on 26 March 1919.

#+#+#+#+#+#+#+#+#+#+#+#+#+#+#

G. GEOFFREY BROWN was born at Brooklyn, N.Y. on 7 March 1941, son of Norman Robert and Kathleen (LaCoy) Brown. He served in the U.S. Navy 1959-1963. On 9 Nov 1968 he married Karen Zeman. She was born at Baltimore, Md. on 15 Feb 1943, the daughter of Edward Joseph and Mildred Elizabeth (Langlotz) Zeman. Mr. Brown attended one year of college and two years of x-ray training. He is now employed as an x-ray technician.

#+#+#+#+#+#+#+#+#+#+#+#+#+#+#

GEORGE C. BROWN was born in Brentwood, N.H. (M) on 18 Aug 1875. He was the son of Benjamin B. and Elizabeth (Thompson) Brown (M). He died at the Exeter (N.H.) Cottage Hospital on 21 Aug 1922 (D). On 1 April 1902 he married Mae Lee at Haverhill, Mass. (M). It was the first marriage for both (M). May Lee was born in Biddeford, Me. (M) on 25 March 1874 (C). She was the daughter of Thomas and May Lee (M). She died at Exeter, N.H. on 28 May 1912 (D).

In 1880 at age five George C. Brown was living with his parents in Brentwood, N.H. (USC). In 1902 when he married he was a carpenter residing in Exeter. His bride was also a resident of Exeter at that time (M). She had previously lived in Portland, Me. (D). Some records indicate she was born in Portland or North Berwick, Me. About 1907 the family was living on Epping Road in Exeter and George C. Brown was employed as a carpenter (DIR).

On 28 May 1912 at age 37 Mae (Lee) Brown died at their home on Epping Road having been a resident of Exeter for ten years (D). A brief notice of her death appeared in the *Exeter News-Letter* of 31 May 1912. Four years later George C. Brown was residing at 24 Union St. in Exeter (DIR). Following the death of his wife he engaged a housekeeper, a Miss Vickery, to care for the children, and she appears in many family snapshots. He was residing on School St. in Exeter when he died in 1922. The following obituary probably appeared in the *Exeter News-Letter*:

George C. Brown

The Brown Families

George C. Brown died early Monday morning, in his 48th year, at the Cottage Hospital of meningitis. He worked as usual for much of last Friday, when he was suddenly stricken and was forthwith taken to the hospital.

Mr. Brown was born in Brentwood, August 18, 1875, son of Benjamin and Elizabeth (Thompson) Brown, and for 22 years had been a highly esteemed citizen of Exeter. He was a skilled carpenter and contracting builder, and had latterly been busied upon the Cunningham bungalows on High Street. It will be recalled that Mr. Brown recently took down, repaired and replaced the wind damaged statue of "Justice" which surmonts the Town Hall.

He was a man of capacity and sterling worth, industrious, of quiet life, and deservedly held in esteem by all who knew him. He has left two daughters and one son; also four brothers, William Brown, of Auburn, Me.; Benjamin Brown, of Bradford, Mass.; John D. Brown and Andrew Brown, both of Amesbury, Mass., and three sisters, Mrs. Jennie W. Morrison, Mrs. Elizabeth Shipley and Mrs. Isabelle Bartlett, all of Exeter.

The funeral was held at the home on School Street Wednesday afternoon and was conducted by Rev. Dr. James W. Bixler. The attendance was large and there were choice floral tributes in profusion. The bearers were the four brothers.

According to family tradition, George C. Brown adopted the middle name Chester, but only the initial. C. appears on any records we have found. He died intestate and Benjamin Brown of Bradford, Mass. (his brother) was appointed administrator of his estate and guardian fo the four children named below (P). The statement in the obituary that he left only one son is an error. George C. Brown and his wife are buried in the Exeter Cemetery on Linden Street where the inscriptions read:

George C. Brown 18 Aug 1875 - 21 Aug 1922
May Lee, wife of George C. Brown
25 March 1874 - 28 May 1912

BROWN Children:

GERTRUDE ELIZABETH - b. Exeter, N.H. on 22 oct 1902.

MORRILL HOWARD - b. Exeter, N.H. on 29 Nov 1903.

LAWRENCE GEORGE - b. Exeter, N.H. on 7 June 1906.

BEATRICE MAY - b. Exeter, N.H. on 5 June 1910.

47

The Brown Families

GERTRUDE ELIZABETH BROWN was born at Exeter, N.H. on 22 Oct 1902, the daughter of George C. and May (Lee) Brown. She married (1) Harold L. Johnston on 21 July 1928 at Portland, Me. He was born at Bangor, Me. in 1904. They subsequently divorced without issue. She married (2) Myrle E. Bristol at Springvale, Me. on 22 June 1939.

Myrle E. Bristol was born in Hampton, N.H. on 4 Jan 1911, the son of Frank Louis and Leora (Philbrick) Bristol. He was first married to Pauline Weiers of Lead, South Dakota, by whom he had four children, Frances L., Carl M., Edna A., and Paul E. Bristol. Pauline (Weiers) Bristol died in March 1939, an obituary appearing in the *Exeter News-Letter* of 31 March 1939.

Mr. Bristol is an electrician and at one time worked for the Exeter and Hamapton Electric Company. In later years he has operated a variety store in Milford, N.H. where the family now resided about 1970.

BRISTOL children:

Robert Alan - b. Portsmouth, N.H. on 5 Sept 1940.

Dorothy Jean - b. Portsmouth, N.H. on 3 Dec 1941.

#+#+#+#+#+#+#+#+#+#+#+#+#+#+#+#

HELEN EDITH BROWN was born at Amesbury, Mass. on 13 Aug 1914, the daughter of John William and Abbie Edith (Anderson) Brown. She died unmarried at age 37 in Orangeburg, New York after a long illness. She had lived and worked in New York City as a buyer for a large department store for many years. At the time of her death she left one brother, John W. Brown, Jr., of Newburyport, two uncles, Benjamin A. Brown of Amesbury and Oscar A. Anderson of North Easton, Mass., and four aunts, Mrs. Mabel Porter and Mrs. Isabel Reid, both of Amesbury, Mrs. Jane Wells of Worcester, Mass., and Mrs. Frank Mcliff of North Easton, Mass. She was buried in Mt. Prospect cemetery, Amesbury. The bearers were Thomas White, James White, Arthur Bastien, and John Gaida (O).

#+#+#+#+#+#+#+#+#+#+#+#+#+#+#+#

HOWARD G. BROWN was born in Fremont, N.H. on 28 November 1890 (O), the son of Benjamin and Annie (Maynes) Brown (O). He died in Bradford, Mass. on 29 February 1952 (P) and is buried there in Elmwood Cemetery as are his parents. On 25 June 1913 he married Jennie Mildred Watt in the parsonage of the Portland Street Baptist Church in Haverhill, Mass., with the Rev. Robert L. Webb officiating. She was born in Hamilton,

Mass. on 6 October 1888, the daughter of Israel Balch and Carrie (Porter) Watt.

Howard G. Brown removed to Exeter, N.H. with his parents after their home in Fremont burned. He attended school there, and later in 1907, while living with his parents on Epping Road in Exeter, was employed as a printer at Hunt's Print Shop (DIR). He shared the musical talents of many members of the Brown family. He played the clarinet in the Exeter Brass Band. In 1910 Mr. Brown removed to Havrhill, Mass. with his father, and there the two men engaged in carpentry.

Later he became a building contractor and was extensively engaged in public affairs. In 1935 Mr. Brown was elected to the board of assessors. He continued to serve on that board nearly continuously for a dozen years, the final eight as its chairman. He was then appointed district supervisor of municipal taxation for Middlesex and Essex counties in the state tax commissioner's office, a post which he held until his death. He had also served as director and president of the Essex County Assessors Association, and in other volunteer positions with the Red Cross and civil defense programs.

Mr. Brown died suddenly, intestate, and administration of his estate was granted to his widow, Jennie M. Brown on 4 March 1952 (P). She and the two children named below were his only heirs (P).

Mr. Brown was never happier than when he was working around a horse or driving one. Some of the places where he drove harness horses were Lewiston, So. Paris, New Gloucester, Cumberland, Gorham, Fryeburg, and Old Orchard Beach in Maine; Newmarket, Plymouth, Rochester, and Salem, N.H.; Topsfield Fair, the Metropolitan Driving Club in Alston, and Foxboro Raceway in Mass. Peter Kent, Etawah Express, and Holanita were some of his horses.

Jennie Mildred (Watt) Brown graduated from Haverhill High School in 1907. She then worked in the office of a box factory for a few years before her marriage. She died at Haverhill Hospital at the age of ninety-seven, having been a lifelong resident.

BROWN children:

BARBARA MAYNES - b. Haverhill, Mass. on 11 Aug 1915.

BREMNER HOWARD - b. Bradford, Mass. on 4 May 1922.

#+#+#+#+#+#+#+#+#+#+#+#+#+#

ISABEL K. BROWN was born on the farm called *Garrarie* in Glasserton Parish, Wigtonshire, Scotland on 8 April 1864 (B). She was the daughter of Benjamin B. and Elizabeth (Thompson)

Brown (D). She died at Brentwood, N.H. on 6 Nov 1962 (D). On 30 May 1887 she married Frank Herbert Bartlett at Brentwood, N.H. (M).

Frank Herbert Bartlett was born in Kingston, N.H. on 29 Sept 1859, the son of Otis W. Bartlett, farmer, of Danville N.H., and his wife the former Sarah E. Sanborn of East Kingston, N.H. (D). He died at Brentwood, N.H. on 7 Dec 1920 (D).

Isabel K. Brown was living on the farm called *Knock* in Glasserton parish with her parents in 1871 (SC). The following year she came to America with them on the steamship *Olympus*, arriving in Boston, Mass. on 18 April 1872 (PL). In 1880 she was living with her parents in Brentwood (USC). When she married Frank H. Bartlett in 1887 they were both residents of Brentwood where he was a shoemaker (M). The family always resided in Brentwood. Isabel was post mistress of the Brentwood Corner Post office (ENL-20 Sept 1895).

The following obituary for Frank H. Bartlett appeared in the *Exeter News-Letter* of 17 Dec 1920:

> *Relatives, friends and neighbors gathered at the home of Frank H. Bartlett last Friday afternoon, December 10th, to pay their last respects to the one who for nearly sixty years had lived among them. Rev. J.B. Knowles, pastor of the Baptist Church, was the officiating clergyman. The bearers were the brothers of his widow, Isabel Brown Bartlett. They were John D. Brown of Amesbury, Mass., Andrew G. Brown of Atkinson, Benjamin Brown of Bradford, Mass., George C. Brown of Exeter. The beautiful oak casket was surrounded by lovely flowers, silent tokens of love and esteem. He was laid to rest in the cemetery in the center of the town. He leaves to mourn his loss his widow, one daughter, Mrs. Pearl Block, and two grandchildren, Gladys Bartlett Block and Evelyn Block.*
>
> *Mr. Bartlett was born in Kingston sixty-one years ago, the son of Otis Willis and Elizabeth Sanborn Bartlett. He lived there a year and a half when his father moved to Brentwood Corner and built the home where the family has always lived since, and Otis and Frank always could be seen for years working at the shoe-bench in the shop erected by the side of the road.*
>
> *Frank Bartlett was a good neighbor and kind friend to everyone. His fun-loving disposition made him a pleasant companion and neighbor. Although he had not been in good health for a year, it was not realized that the end was so near. When stricken, his wife, who is a very efficient nurse, was summoned and all that loving hands could do was done for him. It was particularly pleasing to some that his children were with him in his last years, for the writer of*

Isabelle K. (Brown) Bartlett

The Brown Families

this article distinctly remembers the care given to his
parents by himself and his wife. He will be missed in the
home, neighborhood and town.

Subsequently Isabel Brown Bartlett wrote the folowing will:

Be it known that I, Isabel Brown Bartlett of Brent-
wood, in the County of Rockingham, and State of New
Hampshire, being of sound mind and memory, do make this
my last will and testament in manner and form following:

1st. After the payment of my just debts and legal
expenses of administering the same, I give and bequeath
to my daughter Pearl Block of Brentwood, all my personal
estate of every kind and nature and whereever situate and
found.

2nd. My real estate in Fremont and in Brentwood and
whatever rest I may die seized of, I give and bequeath
and devise unto my daughter Pearl Bartlett Block, for her
use and income during her life, and at her death, my said
estate is to be equally divided between such of my grand-
children as may survive her.

3rd. I constitute and appoint my said daughter, Pearl
Bartlett Block as sole executor of this my last will and
testament hereby revoking any and all wills by me hereto-
fore made.

In witness whereof I have hereunto set my hand and
seal this 19th day of April, 1922.

Signed: Isabel Brown Bartlett

Witnesses: Henry E. Shute, Doris MacKenzie, Arthur
O. Fuller.

Isabel Brown Bartlett lived many years after writing this will
and was a very active member of the Brentwood Baptist Church
as noted in the following item from the *Exeter News-Letter* of 6
September 1945:

Mrs. Isabel B. Bartlett was able to attend the morning
sevice at the Brentwood Baptist Church last Sunday, the
first time since the death of her grandson, Gordon R.
Block, who was killed in the Philippine Islands when his
airplane was shot down. He held very high honors. Mrs.
Block accompanied her mother, and is recovering from her
illness. Mrs. Bartlett, 81 years young, seldom has been
absent a Sunday from her Sunday school class previous to
April.

Following the death of Isabel Brown Bartlett the will above
was filed with the Probate Court by the Exectrix, but it was

never probated, presumably because it was superfluous after forty years. The real estate mentioned had already been bequeathed to Pearl Bartlett Block on her mother's death by the terms of the will of her grandfather, Otis Bartlett (P).

BARTLETT child:

Etta Pearl - b. Brentwood, N.H. on 28 Dec 1889.

#+#+#+#+#+#+#+#+#+#+#+#+#+#+#+#

ISABELL WISEMAN BROWN was born in Amesbury, Mass. on 26 July 1904, the daughter of John D. and Elizabeth (Elliott) Brown. She married (1) Hartwell Reid in Portsmouth, N.H. He was born in Amesbury, Mass. on 21 Jan 1898, the son of James A. Reid from Nova Scotia and his wife, the former Elizabeth Berry from Portland, Me. He died on 16 Dec 1950 while a resident of Salisbury, Mass. Mr. Reid had served on a destroyer in World War I combating the German U-boats in the North Atlantic. Later he worked in automobile plants, and served for a time on the Amesbury police force. He was also a talented musician and with several local bands. At his death he left one son, James, his parents, and one sister, Mrs. Harold Joudrey all of Amesbury, Mass.

Administration of his estate was granted to the widow, Isabell W. Reid (P). The only heir mentioned in the estate, aside from the widow, is the son named below (P).

Subsequently, the widow Isabell married (2) Chester Rohr at Portsmouth, N.H. They made their home in Ft. Lauderdale, Fla. where she died in 1977 leaving, besides her husband, a son, James E. Reid, and a sister, Mrs. Mabel Porter, both of Amesbury, a brother, Benjamin A. Brown of Albuquerque, N.M., four grandchildren and three great-grandchildren. She was buried in Mt. Prospect Cemetery in Amesbury. The pall bearers were James Reid, Jr., Thomas Reid, Daniel Zoeller, James White, William Evans, and Hawley Patten.

REID child:

James Elliott - b. Newburyport, Mass. on 20 Sept 1924.

#+#+#+#+#+#+#+#+#+#+#+#+#+#+#+#

ISABELLA BROWN was born in Glasserton Parish, Wigtonshire, Scotland, on 3 May 1863, the daughter of William and Isabella (Kennedy) Brown (B). She died at Fall River, Mass. on 17 Feb 1903 (D). On 14 Feb 1883 she married William North Wheelock at Hampton Falls, N.H. in a ceremony conducted by

The Brown Families

Rev. I.J. Burgess of the Baptist Church there (M). William North Wheelock was born at Nicteaux Falls, Nova Scotia on 6 June 1863, the son of Major Cleveland and Mary Lois (North) Wheelock (KGW). He died in Fall River, Mass, 2 Sept 1920 (D).

Isabella Brown was born on the farm called *Caindoon* in Glasserton Parish (B) where her father had been employed for several years (SC). She came to America in 1870 with her parents on the steamship *Palmyra* arriving in Boston, Mass. on April 18th of that year (PL). She was nearly 7 years old at the time. The family settled in Hampton Falls shortly after arriving in this country, and Isabella is listed with them there in the 1870 census (USC). She is missing from the family listing in the 1880 census of Hampton Falls (USC). Perhaps she was employed in Providence R.I. where she was residing when she married in 1883 (M).

William North Wheelock removed from Nova Scotia to Lawrence, Mass. with his parents between the years 1865 and 1869 (KGW). The family appears to have remained there permanently, seven of his eight younger siblings having been born there (KGW). In 1883 when he married Isabella Brown he gave his residence as Providence, R.I. and his occupation as blacksmith (M). That was the trade he followed most of his life (D). He later settled his famly in Fall River, Mass. where he operated blacksmith shops for many years. In 1912 he had shops there at 568 Rodman St. and 765 Qkuequechau St. (DIR).

Isabella (Brown) Wheelock died in 1903 while the family resided at 1706 Strafford Rd in Fall River (D). He then married (2) Susan Richmond Borden in April 1904. She was born 12 Aug 1859, probably in Fall River, and died in 1942. William North Wheelock died at the residence on Strafford Road in 1920 having been a resident of that city for about 32 years (D).

WHEELOCK children:

Andrew Leroy - b. in Hampton Falls, N.H. on 13 April 1884 (KGW).
Major William - b. Fall River, Mass. on 22 July 1887 (KGW).
Frank Norman - b. Fall River, Mass. on 30 May 1889 (KGW).
Jennie May - b. Fall River, Mass. on 23 May 1891 (KGW).

Mary Isabel - b. Fall River, Mass. on 19 Jan 1900 (KGW).

#+#+#+#+#+#+#+#+#+#+#+#+#+#

JAMES HOWARD BROWN was born in Wolfeborough, N.H. on 21 May 1945, the son of Morrill Howard and Elva Lillian

(Hersey) Brown. On 7 June 1975 he was married at All Saints Episcopal Church on Wolfeborough to Judith Ann Mulvey of Wolfeborough. She was born there 28 May 1949, the daughter of Robert and Jeannie (Paolucci) Mulvey.

Judith was a graduate of Kingswood Regional High School in Wolfeborough and the Chandler School for Women. She was later employed at the M.S.T. Data Corp. in Braintree, Mass.

James graduated from Brewster Academy in 1963 and entered the University of New Hampshire from which he graduated with a degree in Chemical Egineering. While there he belonged to the *Tau Kappa Epsilon* fraternity. Following his graduation he was employed by the Monsanto Chemical Company in Springfield, Mass. until the fall of 1968 when he entered graduate school at the University of Massachusetts in Amherst where he studied for his Ph.D. degree. He worked for the Badger Company of Cambridge, Mass., and later was employed in northern Virginia. His interests have included motorcycling and competative sports. He also enjoys music and plays the guitar.

#+#+#+#+#+#+#+#+#+#+#+#+#+#

JANE BROWN was born in Ireland (SC), probably in County Down, on 15 June 1839 and died at North Hampton, N.H. on 18 July 1922 (D). She was the daughter of William and Isabella (Kennedy) Brown (D). On 12 April 1864 she married William Whenal on the farm called *Craigdhu* in Glasserton Parish, Wigtonshire, Scotland after banns according to the Church of Scotland (M). She was his second wife.

William Whenal was born in the Parish of Glenluce, Scotland, on 7 Oct 1836 and was batized there on 29 Jan 1837 by the Rev. John Macdowall (PR). He was the natural son of Peter Whannel and Sarah Coburn (PR). In the Scottish records the name is usually spelled Whanel while in the United States it is usually spelled Whenal. Some later records give his mother's name as Cockburn. William Whenal died in North Hampton, N.H. on 9 Oct 1893 (D).

Jane Brown moved from Ireland to Scotland with her parents sometime between 1846 and 1849 as can be deduced from the birth places of her brothers and sisters as given in the Scottish census records. In 1851 she was living with her parents on the farm called *Stellock* in Glasserton Parish, Wigtonshire, Scotland. A decade later she was no longer living at home, but was probably the Jane Brown who was a kitchen maid in the household of William Smith on the farm called *Craighdu* in Glasserton Parish (SC). Her brother Robert Brown was apparently employed as a ploughman in the same household (SC).

In 1841 William Whannel, aged 3, born in Wigtonshire was living on Main Street in Glenluce in the household of Mary

Jane (Brown) Whenal

The Brown Families

Johnstone (SC). There were also three young boys with the surname Coburn living there (SC). Ten years later he was living on the same street with a family named Martin and was described as an orphan (SC). William Whenal married (1) in Whithorn Parish, Wigtonshire, Scotland, Agnes Dickey, aged 26, of Whithorn (M). In that record Peter Whanel, father of William, is described as a deceased farm laborer and William's mother's name is given as Sarah Cockburn (M). Agnes Dickey was the Daughter of Adam Dickey, tinsmith, and Agnes Hamilton (M).

When he first married in 1860, William Whenal was a farm servant on the farm called *Balcray* (M). The following year the census shows him as a ploughman on the farm called *Balsmith* Where he was living with his wife Agnes in Cothouse (SC). They had two children after which she died. In the graveyard of the Priory of Whithorn in Wigtonshire, Scotland, stands a gravestone which reads:

> *Erected by Adam Dickey of Whithorn to the memory of his son George Dickey who died 20 April 1830 age 1 year, 10 months; also his daughter Agnes who died 14 April 1863 age 29 years; also his wife Agnes Hamilton who died 17 April 1866 age 53 years...*

In 1864 when William Whenal married (2) Jane Brown, he was a ploughman on *High Ersock* in Glasserton Parish (M). In that record his father, Peter Whannel, is described as a ploughman and his mother's surname is given as Cockburn; both were deceased (M).

William Whenal brought his family to America in 1870. They arrived in Boston, Mass. on 18 April of that year aboard the steamship *Palmyra* after a passage from Liverpool, England (PL). They appear on the passenger list as follows:

Wm.	Whanell	30	laborer
Jane	"	30	-
Wm.	"	7	-
Robt.	"	5	-
Agnes	"	2	-
John	"	1	-

They came steerage class along with William Brown and his family (PL).

In the 1870 census of Hampton Falls, N.H. the Whenal family was residing in a house with William Brown, Jane's father, and his family. Although the Whenal name is badly mispelled, the family is easily identified by the given names and ages of the family members (USC):

William Quanlle		28	farm laborer	b. Scotland
Jane	"	26	housekeeper	"
Wm. G.	"	7	school	"
Robert	"	4	-	"
Agnes J.	"	2	-	"
John	"	11/12	-	"

The census records also indicated that William and Jane were illiterate, which together with the Scottish accent may explain the mispelling of their name, and that John was born in June (USC).

William Whenal became a United States citizen when he was naturalized before the Supreme Court in Exeter, N.H. on 13 Feb 1878 (N). By 1879 the family had removed to North Hampton, N.H. because on 20 March of that year we find William Whenal of North Hampton buying 2 1/2 acres of pasture land in that town from Juliana and Simon H. Leavitt, also of North Hampton, for $160 (DD). The following year William Whenal bought 194 rods of pasture and woodland, *"with the dwelling house thereon"*, from the same parties (DD). This latter property was bounded by the Lafayette Road in North Hampton (DD). In this latter deed the Leavitts reserved to themselves, *"all the trees on said lot and the priviledge to let them stand as long as we wish"* (DD).

In 1880 the family appeared in the census in North Hampton, N.H. as follows:

William Whenell		35	head	farm laborer	b. Scot.
Jane B.	"	35	wife	housekeeper	"
William G.	"	17	son	farm laborer	"
Robert	"	13	son	-	"
Agnes G.	"	12	dau	school	"
John	"	10	son	"	"
Thomas	"	8	son	"	N.H.
Sarah B.	"	6	son(?)	-	"
Lewis C.	"	4	son	-	"
Lydia M.	"	8/12	dau	-	"

The census also indicates that Robert Whenal was suffering spasms as a result of a fall, and that Lydia M. was born in October (USC).

William Whenal died intestate in 1893. His widow Jane and several of their children petitioned the Probate Court to appoint Francis R. Drake of North Hampton, N.H. as administrator of the estate (P). This was done with Nathaniel Drake and John F. French, both of North Hampton being surties on 17 Oct 1893 (P). Since William Whenal left minor children over the age of 14 those children were permitted to select their own guardian. On

The Brown Families

16 Jan 1894 Louis C. Whenal, Sarah B. Whenal, and Lydia M. Whenal, all over age 14, and all children of William Whenal, chose their brother, John Whenal, to be their legal guardian (P). The widow Jane Whenal continued to live in North Hampton. She was there in 1907 when she wrote her will (P), and was residing there on Lafayette Road with her son Robert about 1916 (DIR). She died there on 18 July 1922 at age 83 after having been a resident for about 52 years (D). The will of Jane (Brown) Whenal reads as follows:

In the name of God Amen. I Jane Whenal of North Hampton, in the County of Rockingham and State of New Hampshire, being of sound and disposing mind and memory, make and publish and declare my last will and testament as follows:

First. I give my son William G. Whenal of Greenland the sum of one dollar and two pillows, one picture (A Surburban Retreat).

Second. I give my son John Whenal, of North Hampton, the sum of one dollar, one desk, one cookstove, one straw matting in the chamber upstairs, one Highland picture for Martin W. Whenal.

Third. I give my son Thomas B. Whenal, of North Hampton, the sum of one dollar, his father's watch, and one white bedstead and spring, two pillows and one picture of Christ in Jerusalem.

Fourth. I give to my daughter Agnes J. Dearborn, wife of George Dearborn the sum of one dollar, my kitchen side table, three kitchen chairs, one parlor rocking chair, one looking glass, one washing machine, one picture (Winter Scene) for Mabel J. Dearborn.

Fifth. I give to my daughter Sarah B. Coffin, wife of Frank Coffin, the sum of one dollar, one featherbed, one bureau, one looking glass, three kitchen chairs, one parlor rocking chair. Picture of my son Lewis, and one buggy robe.

Sixth. I give to my son Robert Whenal of North Hampton all my hens and other poultry, one horse sled, one horse cart, one big hay rack, one work harness, one looking glass, one kitchen clock, two kitchen lamps, one stove, one horse blanket, one large rocking chair in kitchen, the bedstead mattress, bed clothing and all furniture in his bedroom, with exception of desk.

Seventh. I give to my daughter Lydia M. Whenal four flat irons, two tubs, one wringer, all my pressure cans and pickle crocks, all my pantry utensils including all dishes, knives, forks, and spoons, one large posline kittle, one nickle and one iron kittle, two iron pots, one wash

57

boiler, one two seated pung, one buffalo robe, one sewing machine, one six-foot living room table, one cot, one nickle lamp, all my table linens and towels, and one green chest. All my chamber set including bedstead, mattress, spring and bed-clothes, also one other bed matress, spring and bureau. Three other pillows, all my crockery and silverware, all furniture in parlor including bric-a-brac, carpet and pictures etc not otherwise disposed of, all curtains and draperies, one large picture of her father and two large pictures of her grandfather and grandmother.

Eighth. I give to my three daughters, Agnes, Sarah, and Lydia all the rest of my clothing to be divided among them.

Ninth. I give, devise and bequeath to my son Robert Whenal and my daughter Lydia M. Whenal the Shaw Field, so called, near Cemetery in No. Hampton aforesaid share and share alike heirs and assigns forever.

Tenth. All the rest and residue of my estate both personal and real, I give devise and bequeath to my dau. Lydia M. and my son Robert share and share alike after paying my just bills and funeral expenses and I direct that so much of this residue be sold by my executor hereinafter named as is necessary to bring a sum of money sufficient to pay these expenses.

Eleventh. I constitute and appoint my daughter Lydia M. Whenal sole executrix of this will.

In witness whereof I have hereunto set my hand and seal this fifteenth day of July 1907.

Signed, Jane Whenal (her mark)

Witnesses: Alberta Berry, Annie F. Perry, and Llewellyn F. Hobbs.

The will was proved on 21 Aug 1922 on petition of Lydia W. Lane, formerly Lydia M. Whenal, of North Hampton, N.H. the Executrix named therein (P).

The death of Jane Whenal was rcorded in the *Exeter News-Letter* of Friday July 21, 1922 as follows:

The death of Mrs. Jane Whenal, widow of William H. Whenal occured at her home on the Lafayette Road, Tuesday evening after a brief illness.

Mrs. Whenal was 83 yrs of age, a native of Scotland, but had resided in North Hampton for over 50 years. She is survived by 4 sons, William G., of Greenland (N.H.); and Robert, John and Thomas B. of North Hampton; 3 daughters, Mrs. George Dearborn, Mrs. Frank Coffin, and Mrs Howard Lane, all of Hampton; 3 brothers, John, William, and Andrew Brown all of Hampton Falls; and 2 sisters, Mrs.

The Brown Families

Joseph Drysdale of Hampton Falls, and Mrs. Alonzo Jenness, of Amesbury, Mass.

The funeral was held from her late home, Friday afternoon at 2 o'clock, Rev. William L. Linaberry officiating.

Albert Locke, Arthur E. Seavey, Justin E. Drake, and Austin W. Norton acted as bearers. Interment was in Central Cemetery.

The following obituary appeared in the *Exeter News-Letter* on Friday August 4, 1922:

On July 18 occured the death of Mrs. Jane Whenal, widow of William Whenal, at her home on the Lafayette Road in North Hampton, N.H. Mrs. Whenal will be remembered as a good neighbor, always doing for others in time of sickness and where help was needed. She was a member of the Congregational Church for about 50 years, and attended as long as she was able. She was a kind and loving mother, and her children deeply mourn her loss, and her place in that home can never be filled. Mrs. Whenal had just passed her 83rd birthday. She is survived by 4 sons, William G., of Greenland; Robert, John and Thomas B. of North Hampton. Three daughters, Mrs. George Dearborn, Mrs Frank Coffin, and Mrs. Howard M. Lane, all of Hampton.

The funeral was held from her late home on Friday with a large gathering of relatives and friends to pay their last respects to one they held in high esteem. The floral tributes were many and beautiful.

William Whenal and his wife Jane are buried in the cemetery on Post Road near the junction with New Road in North Hampton where the inscriptions read:

```
William Whenal d.  9 Oct 1893 ae. 62y. 4m.
Jane Brown, wife of William Whenal
     b.  15 June 1839 - d.  18 July 1922.
```

WHENAL children by Agnes Dickey:

Sarah Dickey - b. 24 May 1861 at *Balsmith*, Whithorn Parish, Wigtonshire, Scotland (B). Probably died young since she is not on the passenger list with the family (PL).
William George - b. 6 March 1863 at *Balsmith*, Whithorn Parish, Wigtonshire, Scotland (B).

59

The Brown Families

WHENAL children by Jane Brown:

Robert - b. 2 Feb 1865 on *High Ersock*, Glasserton Parish,
    Wigtonshire, Scotland (B).
Agnes Jane - b. 7 April 1867 on *High Ersock*, Glasserton
    Parish, Scotland (B).
John - b. June 1869 on *High Ersock*, Glasserton Parish,
    Scotland (B).
Thomas Benjamin - b. 16 Jan 1872 at North Hampton, N.H.
    (D).
Sarah Belle - b. 31 Oct 1874 at North Hampton, N.H.(D).

Louis C. - b. 8 May 1877 at North Hampton, N.H. (B).

Lydia May - b. 1 Oct 1879 at North Hampton, N.H. (D).

#+#+#+#+#+#+#+#+#+#+#+#+#+#+#+#

JENNIE W. BROWN was born in Brentwood, N.H. (M) on 6
June 1872, the daughter of Benjamin B. and Elizabeth (Thompson) Brown (FR), shortly after the family arrived from Scotland
(PL). She died in Exeter, N.H. on 1 Dec 1937 (D). She married
(1) William H. Burke; (2) Oscar Morrison; (3) William C. Sweetland.

Jennie W. Brown was living with her parents in Brentwood,
N.H. in 1880 and was attending school (USC). She was still a
resident of Brentwood when she married William H. Burke there
on 12 Oct 1888 at the age of 16 (M). He was born in Canada (M)
on 21 April 1867 (C), the son of William P. Burke a brick
manufacturer also born in Canada (C). His mother was a school-
teacher named Levinia Constant.

William H. Burke worked at his father's brickyard in Epping,
N.H. as a young man. In the *Exeter News-Letter* of 21 Feb 1890
under the Epping news we read *W.P. Burke has about 20 teams
drawing wood to his brickyard.* When he married in 1880, William H. Burke was residing in Fremont and gave his occupation
as "trader" (M). He died on 27 Dec 1890 (C) while a resident of
Epping, N.H. where he was proprietor of a men's clothing store
(P). His widow was pregnant with their first child, a daughter
born about a month after his death. William H. Burke was
buried in the Sleeper Cemetery on Martin Rd. off County Farm
Rd. in Fremont, N.H. where the inscription reads:

Wm. H. Burke b. 21 April 1867 d. 27 Dec 1890

On 20 Dec 1893 Jennie W. Burke married Oscar Morrison at
Brentwood, N.H. (M). He was born in Canada (M), probably in

Trois Rivers, Quebec, on 27 Sept 1866 (C). He was the son of John and Lenore Morrison (M). His parents were born in Canada in 1848 and 1845, respectively, and were still residing there in 1893 (M). Oscar Morrison was a clerk residing in Epping, N.H. in 1893 when he married Jennie (Brown) Burke (M). It was his first marriage and her second (M). In 1907 the couple was residing at 49 Main St. in Exeter, N.H. with her daughter Jennie Mae Burke, and two younger children. They subsequently separated. By 1916 Oscar Morrison had removed to Haverhill, Mass., but Jennie remained at the Main St. address in Exeter (DIR).

Oscar Morrison died in Haverhill as a result of a fall down a flight of stairs. He died intestate leaving as heirs, daughter Helen F. Morrison of Exeter, N.H., and son Oscar L. Morrison of Kittery, Me. (P). The former was granted administration of the estate (P). His death is noted in the following item from the *Exeter News-Letter* of 29 April 1927:

> *Mr. Oscar Morrison, of Haverhill, Mass., a former resident of Exeter, died at the Gale Hospital, April 17, from a fractured skull received two weeks ago previous. Interment was in the family lot in Newmarket.*

Inscriptions from the Calvary Cemetery at Rockingham Junction in Newmarket, N.H. read as follows:

Oscar Morrison b. 27 Sept 1866 d. 17 April 1927
Lillian A. Morrison b. 22 Feb 1895 d. 23 Aug 1895

At age fifty-one the widowed Jennie Morrison married William C. Sweetland on 20 April 1929 at Portsmouth, N.H. where he resided, and was employed as a chauffeur, at age forty-three. He was born in Everett, Mass., ths son of George and Charlotte (Hookey) Sweetland of England (M). She died in Exeter in 1937 having been a resident of the town for about 40 years (D). The following obituary in which her name is erroneously given as Jane, appeared in the *Exeter News-Letter* of 3 Dec 1937:

> *Mrs. Jane (sic) W. Sweetland, wife of Willaim C. Sweetland, died at her home on Main Street on Wednesday morning, after a long illness. Mrs. Sweetland was born in Brentwood, June 6, 1872. She was the youngest daughter of the late Benjamin B. Brown and Elizabeth Thompson Brown. She had lived in Exeter for the past forty years.*
>
> *Besides her husband, she is survived by three children: Mrs. George E. Dearborn, and Miss Helen F. Morrison, of Exeter; and O. Linwood Morrison, of Kittery, Maine, and three grandchildren. She also leaves two sisters, Mrs. Frank Bartlett of Brentwood, and Mrs. Wilbur A. Shipley of*

The Brown Families

Merrimac, Mass. Also three brothers: Benjamin Brown of Bradford, Mass., and John and Andrew of Amesbury, Mass.

Funeral services will be held from the home on Main Street at two-thirty o'clock, Friday. Burial will be in Exeter.

BURKE child:

Jennie Mae – b. Brentwood, N.H. on 24 Jan 1891 (P).

MORRISON children:

Lillian Ardella – b. 22 Feb 1895 (C).

Oscar Linwood – b. Exeter, N.H. on 12 March 1899.

Helen Fern – b. Exeter, N.H. on 15 Nov 1900.

#+#+#+#+#+#+#+#+#+#+#+#+#+#+#

JOHN BROWN was born in Glasserton Parish, Wigtonshire, Scotland (SC) on 27 July 1849, son of William and Isabella (Kennedy) Brown (M). He died in Anna Jacques Hospital in Newburyport, Mass. on 12 Aug 1931. On 28 Dec 1877 he married Mary P. Tarleton at Hampton Falls, N.H. in a ceremony conducted by I.J. Burgess of that town (M). She was the daughter of William and Caroline (Palmer) Tarleton (M). Mary P. Tarleton was born in Hampton Falls on 11 March 1856 and died there on 6 Jan 1931.

John Brown came to America as a young man, but the exact date of his arrival is uncertain. According to family tradition he came over with his older brother, Robert. John Brown was naturalized before the Circut Court in Dover, N.H. on 8 March 1876, and those records indicate that he arrived in the United States in June of 1868 (N). However, the corresponding records of his brother Robert state that Robert arrived on 16 June 1869 (N). We cannot say which record is correct, if indeed they did come together as seems probable, but are inclined to place more credence in the former record, since it was made much sooner after their arrival (N).

In 1870 John Brown was a farm laborer living at home with his parents in Hampton Falls (USC). When he married in 1877 he gave his occupation as laborer (M). In the 1880 census he and his wife Mary were living in North Hampton where they were enumerated as follows:

```
John Brown   head   30   farm laborer   b. Scotland
Mary P. "    wife   24   housekeeper    b. N.H.
```

John & Mary P. (Tarleton) Brown

The Brown Families

They later removed to a farm in Hampton Falls where they lived the rest of their lives in a house that had been built in 1852 by Samuel Palmer, grandfather of Mary P. (Tarleton) Brown (HF). John Brown had a team of horses with which he was employed in the construction of the electric car tracks between Hampton and Exeter, N.H. which went into service in 1897 (HF).

Mary P. Brown died in January of 1931. The following notice of her death appeared in the *Exeter News-Letter* of 9 Jan 1931:

HAMPTON FALLS - the death of Mary, wife of John A. Brown, occurred early Tuesday morning at the family home, following an illness of several weeks. Mrs Brown was in her 76th year, and was born in Hampton Falls, the daughter of William and Caroline (Palmer) Tarleton. She is survived by the widower and one daughter, Maude, also two brother, George, who made his home with her, and John, who lives in Hampton. Mrs. Brown had been a member of the Baptist Church for many years and was a most estimable woman. She was a great lover of home and one who looked well to the ways of her household. She was devoted wife and mother and a kind neighbor. She will be much missed by a large circle of friends.

The Union (Woman's Christian Temperance Union) has lost another valued member in the death of Mrs. Mary P. Brown. We offer our sympathy to the bereaved family.

The day before his wife died John Brown made the following will:

Be it known hereby, that I, John Brown of Hampton Falls, in the County of Rockingham and State of New Hampshire, do make and publish this my LAST WILL AND TESTAMENT.

After the payment of my just debts, funeral charges and expenses of Administration, I dispose of my estate as follows:-

All the residue of my estate of what I may be possessed at the time of my decease, real, personal, and mixed, where ever it may be found and of whatsoever it may consist I give and bequeath to my daughter, Maude A. Brown.

I hereby request that appointment of my said daughter, Maude A. Brown, as Executor of this my last will and testament.

In testimony whereof, I here unto set my hand, this 5th day of January, in the year one thousand nineteen hundred and thirty-one.

The Brown Families

Signed: John Brown
Witnesses: George M. Tarleton, Jennie S. James, Ernest C. Cole.

Following the death of John Brown in August of 1931 the following obituary appeared in the Exeter News-Letter of 21 Aug 1931:

> *HAMPTON FALLS - The death of John Brown at the age of 82 years and 17 days has removed from the Church (Baptist) a valued deacon who has occupied that position many years. He had lived in this country 62 years. At one time he was employed at the Farragut House (Rye Beach, N.H.). For many years he carried shoes to local shoemakers and returned them when finished to Haverhill, Mass. In his late life he had been successful in raising tomato and other early vegetable plants for market. His brother-in-law, George Tarleton, assisted him in this pursuit. Last January Mrs. Brown died, since which time Mr. Brown has been cared for as well as before by his faithful daughter, Miss Maude Brown. His interest in selling vegetables in Seabrook led him into the hearts of many who confided to him their troubles and he knew where to go for assistance as they discovered from his helpfulness. The row of trees in front of the parsonage was planted by him. When the Pastor was ill he baptized Mrs. Mary Janvrin. Members of the Church and faternal organizations attended his funeral Sunday at 2 P.M. His relatives are numerous and to them we extend our deepest sympathy.*

The will shown above was probated on 8 Sept 1931 (P). Maude A. Brown was appointed executrix and William Brown of Hampton was appointed to take inventory of the estate on that same date (P). The William Brown who took the inventory was probably the same William Brown who was engaged as undertaker (P). He was John Brown's, nephew, the son of his brother Robert.

John and Mary P. Brown are buried in High Street Cemetery in Hampton, N.H. where the inscriptions read:

> John Brown 1849-1931
> Mary P. Brown 1856-1931
> George M. Tarleton 1864-1936

BROWN child (adopted):

MAUDE AILEEN - born Hampton, N.H. on 23 July 1888.

The Brown Families

JOHN D. BROWN was born on the farm called *Knock* in Glasserton Parish, Wigtonshire, Scotland on 19 January 1862, the son of Benjamin B. and ELizabeth (Thompson) Brown (B). He died in Amesbury, Mass. on 25 March 1941 and is buried there in Mt. Prospect Cemetery (D). On 20 October 1888 John D. Brown married Elizabeth Elliott at Brentwood, N.H. (M). Elizabeth Elliott was born in Tempo, Ireland on 1 June 1867. She was the daughter of John and Susan Elliott of Ireland (M), who later settled in Exeter, N.H. Elizabeth died in Amesbury, Mass. on 16 April 1933 and is also buried there (D). Elizabeth Elliott had two brothers, John and William, and two sisters, Faith and Margaret, all of whom lived in Exeter.

In 1871 John D. Brown, aged 9 years, was living with his parents on the farm called *Knock* where he was born (SC). He was attending school at the time (SC). The middle initial "D" does not appear in the Scottish records. It was one he adopted as a young man. It appears on his marriage record and other later records. According to tradition it stood for Durgin, but that has not been found on any records.

John D. Brown came to America with his parents on the steamship *Olympus*, arriving in Boston, Mass. on 18 April 1872 (PL). The family took up residence in Brentwood, N.H. shortly thereafter. In 1880 John D. Brown was boarding with the family of William Veasey in Brentwood (USC) where he was employed as a farm laborer. Most of the sons of Benjamin B. Brown were boarded out as farm laborers as young men in order to help support the large family.

John D. Brown was apparently an energetic person; he engaged in a variety of enterprises as the records show. In 1883 while still a young man he bought a 1/4 acre lot with buildings on it from Mary A. Upton for $700.00 (DD). This land in Brentwood, N.H. was surrounded on three sides by his father's property (DD). John D. Brown subsequently sold it in 1885 to George E. Durgin of Dover for $465.00 (DD).

In 1888 when they married John D. Brown and Elizabeth Elliott were both residents of Brentwood, N.H. She is said to have come from Tempo, Ireland when about 13 years of age, perhaps with her parents, but further knowledge of her backgrownd is lacking. John D. Brown described himself as a farmer when he married (M).

On 10 Oct 1891 John D. Brown of Brentwood bought 1 1/2 acres with buildings in Brentwood from David A. Woodman (DD). On 10 Dec 1891 he bought a 13 acre plot with buildings in Brentwood on the west side of the highway from Epping to Kingston (DD). He sold both of these properties to Mary E. Johnson, wife of Moses Johnson of Pelham, N.H. for $1.00 and other considerations (DD). This 13 acre plot bounded on land of Frank H. Bartlett, a brother-in-law.

The Brown Families

It appears that John D. Brown also ran a grocery store in Brentwood for a short time. The following item appeared in the *Exeter News-Letter* of 10 march 1899:

> *The grocery store, built and operated recently by John Brown at Brentwood Corner must be greatly appreciated by people in that vicinity.*

He also operated a milk business in Brentwood as noted in this item from the 29 March 1901 *Exeter News-Letter*:

> *Walter H. Lyford has purchased the milk carrying business of John D. Brown.*

Apparently the grocery business was not entirely satisfactory because in the *Exeter News-letter* of 12 April 1901 we find under the Brentwood news:

> *John Brown, grocer, at Brentwood Corner, is not closing out his business with view to removal from town as stated in the correspondence last week. He had thought that the sale of his business was as good as made, but the deal fell through. He is still in business at the old stand.*

The family shortly thereafter removed to Amesbury, Mass. where they lived for about 40 years (D-John D. Brown). John D. Brown learned carpentry and is said to have built the first carriage body for Dearborn's Express Co. of Exeter, N.H. which was then owned and operated by George E. Dearborn. When he died in 1941 John D. Brown was described as a self-employed building contractor (D).

The Brown's home at 7 Myrtle St. in Amesbury, Mass. was a focal point for the family for many years. John D. was known as Old John, his son John was referred to as Young John, and his grandson John was called Little John in order to keep them straight at the family gatherings. John D. Brown's parents resided with him in Amesbury during their final years (O-Benj. B. Brown).

In the will dated 30 March 1929 Elizabeth J. Brown bequeathed her entire estate to her husband, John D. Brown, and named him Executor (P). Following her death in 1933 the following obituary appeared in an unidentified paper:

> *Mrs. Elizabeth J. Brown, wife of John D. Brown, died at her home at 7 Myrtle Steet, Amesbury, Mass., after a short illness. She was for many years a resident of this town. She leaves as survivors two sons, John W. and Benjamin A., and four daughters, Ella M. White, Lena J.*

66

A Brown Family Gathering in Amesbury, Mass.

Benjamin, Mabel F., Annie (Maynes), Elizabeth (Elliot),
John D., Gertrude E., George C., Andrew G.,
Beatrice M. (child)

John D. & Elizabeth (Elliot) Brown

Mabel F. Brown, Gertrude E. Brown, Beatrice M. Brown

The Brown Families

Wells, Mabel F. Porter, and Isabelle W. Reid. The funeral was held from her home at 7 Myrtle Street on Wednesday afternoon at two-thirty.

The following notices appeared in the *Amesbury Daily News* issues of 16 April and 20 April 1933, respectively:

Mrs. John Brown Passed Away At Noon On Sunday - On Sunday, following a very brief illness, Mrs. Elizabeth J. Brown passed away at the family home, No. 7 Myrtle Street, at the noon hour.

Mrs. Brown has resided in our town for a number of years and had many friends. It was also her priviledge tohave quite a large family, there being two boys, B. Alexander and John W., and four girls, Mrs. Thomas B. White, Mrs. Carlton L. Wells, Mrs. Mabel Porter, and Mrs. Hartwell Reid, also one sister and one brother all of whom survive her.

Funeral services will be held from the home on Wednesday afternoon at 2:30.

Funeral Services Of Mrs. John Brown Largely Attended - Yesterday afternoon at 2:30 a large number of relatives and freinds gathered at the home of the late Mrs. Elizabeth J. Brown, wife of John D. Brown, where funeral services for her were held. There were also an unusually large number of very beautiful floral tributes.

Rev. S. James Cann, minister of the Portland Street Baptist CVhurch, Haverhill, and formerly of this town was the officiating clergyman and paid a splendid tribute to her life and character. Wm. H. Graves sang two splendid sepections, "Beautiful Isle of Somewhere" and "The Old Rugged Cross."

B. Alexander Brown, John W. Brown, Carlton L. Wells, Thomas B. White, and Hartwell Reid were the bearers.

Interment was in the family lot in Mt. Prospect Cemetery where a committal service was held.

The arrangements were in charge of Pillsbury and Gale, undertakers.

John D. Brown wrote a will dated 2 Jan 1936 and a codicil dated 3 July 1936 in which he bequeathed his estate in equal shares to the children named below, execpt for the two girls who died young (P). His son-in-law Carlton L. Wells, then of Philadelphia, Pa. was named Executor (P).

Following the death of John D. Brown in 1841 the two notices below appeared in the *Amesbury Daily News* issues of 26 March and 29 March, 1941, respectively:

67

The Brown Families

John D. Brown of 7 Myrtle St., a resident of this town for the past 39 years, pased away (Friday, 28 March) at the family home last evening, after several months of failing health, at the age of 79 years, two months, and six days. Mr. Brown was born in Glasiton (sic), Scotland, coming to this country when a young man.

He was a carpenter by trade and completed many projects as a contractor. He served this town as superintendent of streets for two years. Mr. Brown's wife, Elizabeth J. (Elliott) died in 1933. During his lifetime in Amesbury he made many friends.

Funeral services for John D. Brown, 7 Myrtle Street, were held yesterday afternood at 2 o'clock at the Pillsbury and Gale Funeral Home, 2 Hillside Avenue. Rev. David Buzzell, pastor of the Market Street Baptist Church conducted the services. There were many relatives and friends in attendance and a large number of beautiful floral tributes.

John W. Brown, Alexander Brown, Thomas B. White, and Hartwell B. Reid served as bearers. Interment was made in the family lot. Mt. Prospect Cemetery where a commital service was held in charge of Rev. Mr. Buzzell.

He is survived by four daughters, Mrs. Thomas B. White (Ella Margaret), of Amesbury, Mass., Mrs. Carlton L. Wells (Jane), of Worcester, Mass., Mrs. Mabel Porter of Amesbury, Mass., and Mrs. Isabell Reed (sic) of Salisbury, Mass.; two sons, Mr. Benjamin Alexander Brown of Springfield, Mass., and John W. Brown of Watertown, Mass.; two sisters, Mrs. Frank (Isabelle) Bartlett of Brentwood, N.H., and Mrs. Elizabeth Shipley of Merrimac, Mass; two brothers, Andrew G Brown of Amesbury, Mass., and Benjamin B. Brown of Bradford, Mass.; also eight grandchildren and two great grandchildren.

BROWN children:

JOHN WILLIAM - b. Brentwood, N.H. on 30 Nov 1891.

ELLA MARGARET - b. Brentwood, N.H. on 28 Aug 1893.

LENA JANE - b. Brentwood, N.H. on 31 March 1895.

Sarah Belle - b. Brentwood, N.H. on 5 July 1897. She died there aged 1 yr. 2 mos. on 21 Sept 1898 (ENL-13 Jan 1899). Said to be buried in the Brown lot in Brentwood, but there is no gravestone.

The Brown Families

Anna Thompson – b. Brentwood, N.H. on 29 July 1898 (ENL-30 Sept 1898). She died there on 27 Sept 1898 (ENL-13 Jan 1899), and is said to be buried in the Brown lot in Brentwood, although there is no gravestone.

MABEL FAITH – b. Brentwood, N.H. on 27 Dec 1899.

ISABELL WISEMAN – b. Amesbury, Mass. on 26 July 1904.

BENJAMIN ALEXANDER – b. Amesbury, Mass. on 11 Jan 1901.

#+#+#+#+#+#+#+#+#+#+#+#+#+#

JOHN WILLIAM BROWN as born at Brentwood, N.H. on 30 Nov 1891, the son of John D. and Elizabeth (Elliott) Brown. He was employed as a chauffeur by the Studebaker family of Rye Beach, N.H. and the Biddle family of Amesbury, Mass., and was a car salesman for many years in the Boston area. He married (1) Abbie Edith Anderson who was of Swedish extraction. They owned property on Market St. in Amesbury over the period 1928-1934 (P) and lived at 5 Myrtle Street for many years. Abbie died 3 Oct 1933 as noted in the following three items from the *Amesbury Daily News*. The first two are from the issue of 4 Oct 1933 and the last from the issue of 6 Oct 1933:

> *Mrs. Abbie E., wife of John W. Brown, passed away at the family home, 5 Myrtle St., in the late afternoon of yesterday, following a long illness.*
>
> *The deceased was born in Amesbury, Mass., Feb. 6, 1866. Her parents were John A. and Amanda (Gustafson) Anderson.*
>
> *Mrs. Brown was an attendant of the Market Street Baptist Church and a member of the Corner Class. She was also a member of Colfax Rebekah Lodge and had a great many friends.*
>
> *Besides her husband she leaves two children, Miss Helen and Master John A., Jr. Her mother also survives her and one sister, Mrs. Frank Maliff of North Easton, Mass., and one brother, Oscar A. Anderson of Methuen, Mass.*
>
> *Funeral services will be held from the family home Thursday at 2 o'clock.*

> *DEATH NOTICE: BROWN in Amesbury, Mass., Oct. 3, 1933. Mrs. Abbie E. Brown, wife of John W. Brown, age 45 years 7 months and 27 days. Funeral services from the family home 5 Myrtle St., Thursday afternoon at 2 o'clock.*

The Brown Families

Beautiful floral tributes were displayed in an unusual number for the funeral service of Mrs. Abbie E. Brown, wife of John W. Brown, when held from the home at number 5 Myrtle Street of this town yesterday afternoon at 2 o'clock.

Mrs. Brown was a young woman very highly respected and with a great many friends, which was evidenced by the large number of floral pieces.

Rev. Howard E. Koelb, minister of the Market St. Baptist Church was the officiating clergyman. Mr. William H. Graves sang two selections, "The Old Rugged Cross" and "Beautiful Isle of Somewhwere." Alexander Brown, Carlton L. Wells, Thomas B. White, and Frank Maliff served as bearers.

Interment was in the family lot, Mt. Prospect Cemetery, with a comittal service at the grave.

John William Brown was appointed administrator of his wife's estate in 1934 (P), and on 12 Dec 1933 the two surviving children were placed under the guardianship of his sister Mabel Faith (Brown) Porter (P).

Mr. Brown later married (2) Elsie Bishop about whom we know nothing further. The City Clerk's records in Amesbury indicate he died 20 Aug 1946 aged 54 years, 8 months, and 20 days, at Cambridge, Mass., although his daughter reported that he actually died in Waltham. The following three items concerning his death appeared in the *Amesbury Daily News*, the first two from the issue of 21 Aug 1946, and the last from the issue of August 23rd.

DEATHS: BROWN, suddenly in ·Waltham, Mass., August 20, 1946. John W. Brown, husband of Elsie (Bishop) Brown. Funeral from his late home, 177 Chaffee Ave., Waltham, Thursday at 2. Friends invited. Interment at 4 in Mt. Prospect Cemetery, Amesbury, Mass.

The funeral services of John W. Brown, brother of Selectman Benjamin A. Brown, and well known former resident of this town, who died suddenly early yesterday morning will be held from his late home, 177 Chaffee Avenue, Waltham, Mass.

The remains will be brought to Amesbury for interment at 4 in the family lot in Mt. Prospect Cemetery of this town.

Committal services for John W. Brown, former resident of this town were held at Mt. Prospect Cemetery yesterday afternoon at 4, following funeral services at his late home.

The Brown Families

At the services in Waltham there was an unusually large attendance, including many automobile salesmen of Boston's "Motor Row," Commonwealth Avenue, where the deceased was well and favorably known. Ten cars filled with friends and associated of Mr. Brown comprised the funeral cortege which motored from Waltham to Amesbury.

BROWN children:

ALICE LENA - b. Amesbury, Mass., on 26 May 1912.

HELEN EDITH - b. Amesbury, Mass. on 13 Aug 1914.

JOHN WILLIAM - b. probably in Amesbury, Mass., on 12 Apr 1917.

#+#+#+#+#+#+#+#+#+#+#+#+#+#

JOHN WILLIAM BROWN was born 12 Apr 1917, probably in Amesbury, Mass., the son of John William Brown and Abbie Anderson. He served a long hitch in the U.S. Army from which he had retired by 1968. In that year he died suddenly at Fort Sill, Oklahoma and is buried there. He married Eleanor _____ from Newburyport, Mass. Following his death she worked as a nurse at a hospital in Melrose, Mass.

BROWN children:

Greg -

John -

#+#+#+#+#+#+#+#+#+#+#+#+#+#

JOYCE ADELE BROWN was born in Bridgeport, Conn. on 3 Jan 1936, the daughter of Nile Holmes and Emily Louise (DeLong) Brown. She married (1) Leon R. Isabelle and had one daughter. She married (2) Louis Duarte and had one daughter. They resided in Buena Park, Calif. about 1970.

ISABELLE child:

Donna Lee.

DUARTE child:

Lisa Louise - b. 2 July 1969.

The Brown Families

JUDITH LEE BROWN was born in Newbuyrport, Mass. on 20 July 1933, the daughter of Clyde W. and Ruth (Brown) Brown. She married Arthur Prentiss on 13 Sept 1952. He was born in Manchester, N.H. on 14 June 1933. Mr. Prentiss served in the Korean War. He now owns and operates Art's Trucking and Repair Company where Judith Lee is bookkeeper. The family resided at Merrimack, N.H. about 1981.

PRENTISS children:

Linda - b. Manchester, N.H. on 3 October 1953.

David - b. Manchester, N.H. on 29 August 1956.

Mark - b. Manchester, N.H. on 27 June 1966.

Lisa - b. Manchester, N.H. on 17 February 1970.

#+#+#+#+#+#+#+#+#+#+#+#+#+#+#+#+#

LENA JANE BROWN was born in Brentwood, N.H. on 31 March 1895, the daughter of John D. and Elizabeth (Elliott) Brown. She married Carlton L. Wells of a well-known Amesbury family in Philadelphia, Pa., on 24 Dec 1917.

The Amesbury City Clerk's records indicate that Mr. Wells died 15 Feb 1953 aged 69 years, 11 months, and 27 days. Mr. Wells was a graduate of Worcester Tech, and was employed by the Fisher Body Company in Detroit, the Mullen Body Company of Salem Ohio, and later for an extended period by the E. G. Budd Company in Philadelphia. While with the latter company he was sent to England to supervise the construction of an assembly line in a new plant in Oxford. Prior to his retirement he was with the Worcester Pressed Steel Company in Worcester. During WWI he served a five year hitch in the Navy.

Mr. Wells was survived by his wife, Jane (Brown) Wells, and a daughter, Mrs. Virginia Niford (Mrs. Roger Niford), both of Worcester, Mass. Other survivors include a sister, Charlotte Strong of Bermuda, and one aunt, Miss Addie True of Amesbury, Mass.

Following the death of her husband Jane, as she preferred to be called, lived on Hillside Ave. in Amesbury, Mass. until her death on 8 Feb 1976 leaving her daughter, Mrs. Virginia E. Niford, Worcester; a brother, Benjamin A. Brown, Albequerque, N.M.; two sisters, Mrs. Mabel F. Porter, Amesbury, and Mrs. Isobel W. Rohr, Ft. Lauderdale, Fla.; and several nieces and nephews.

Carlton L. & Lena Jane (Brown) Wells

WELLS child (adopted):

Virginia E. - married Roger Niford.

#+#+#+#+#+#+#+#+#+#+#+#+#+#+#

MABEL FAITH BROWN was born in Brentwood, N.H. on 27 Dec 1899, the daughter of John D. and Elizabeth (Elliott) Brown. She married Harold Carey Porter at Newburyport, Mass. on 19 March 1921. He was twenty-four years of age, the son of Edward N. Porter and Annie G. Bridges, both of Newburyport. At the time of their marriage Harold was a clerk, and Mabel was a stenographer. They subsequently divorced. He died 8 Aug 1939 at age 42 years, 9 months, while a resident at 26 Jefferson Street in Newburyport, and is buried there in Bellville Cemetery. After they divorced Mabel returned to Amesbury and took care of her parents. She was bookkeeper for the J. J. Newberry Co. in Amesbury for many years.

PORTER child:

Doris Brown. - b. Newburyport, Mass. on 27 Sep 1921.

#+#+#+#+#+#+#+#+#+#+#+#+#+#+#

MARCIA FRANCES BROWN was born at Haverhill, Mass. on 28 August 1953, the daughter of Bremner Howard and Marica Merrow (McCarthy) Brown. She graduated from Dana Hall and Smith College. She was a Brownie, Girl Scout and Rainbow Girl. She plays piano and studied ballet for several years. She collects dolls and enjoys skiing and swimming.

#+#+#+#+#+#+#+#+#+#+#+#+#+#+#

MARION BEATRICE BROWN born at Marblehead, Mass. on 29 July 1910, the daughter of Clarence Warren and Thannie W. (Gleason) Brown. She died at Concord Hospital on 23 June 1974. She married Norman S. Ewing at Portsmouth, N.H. on 29 July 1932. He was born in Woodland, Me. on 4 April 1908, the son of Randall Seth and Janie Martha Ewing.

Mr. Ewing joined the Marines in 1927, trained at Paris Island, and spent four years in Nicaragua with the 2nd Marine Corps. Later he served with the Seabees in the South Pacific in WWII. He is now a buyer for the Lowell Rendering Co. He is a Past Master of Washington Lodge #61 in Manchester where the family resides. Mr. Ewing is an avid sports fisherman.

Marion Beatrice (Brown) Ewing graduated from high school in 1929 and worked as a telephone operator until her marriage.

She was later employed by the Manchester School System. Mrs. Ewing was a member of Ruth Chapter #16 of the Order of the Eastern Star, and enjoyed sewing and knitting.

EWING children:

Thomas Brown - b. Portsmouth, N.H. on 8 May 1934.

Lynn E. (adopted) - b. Manchester, N.H. on 26 July 1954.

#+#+#+#+#+#+#+#+#+#+#+#+#+#+#+#

MARJORIE LOUISE BROWN was born at Bridgeport, Conn. on 18 Sept 1919, the daughter of Nile Holmes and Emily Louise (DeLong) Brown. She married (1) Willard Brunt, one son; (2) Peter Carreiro, one son; (3) Eugene Conti, no issue. As a young woman Marjorie sang in a trio with her sisters, Bernice and Vivian. They were known as "The Brown Sisters", and appeard on a local radio station. She resided in Pawtucket, R.I. about 1970.

BRUNT child:

Carl Martin - b. Bridgeport, Conn. on 4 Sept 1937.

CARREIRO child:

Peter C. - b. Attleboro, Mass. on 16 Jan 1949.

#+#+#+#+#+#+#+#+#+#+#+#+#+#+#+#

MARTHA BROWN was born in Glasserton Parish, Wigton-shire, Scotland on 9 Dec 1852, the daughter of William and Isabella (Kennedy) Brown (PR). She was baptized there on 12 May 1853 (PR). She died at Amesbury, Mass. on 6 Nov 1922 (D). On 4 Jan 1875 she married Samuel Alonzo Jenness at North Hampton, N.H. in a ceremony conducted by Rev. T. V. Haines of that town (M). Samuel Alonzo Jenness was born at North Hampton, N.H. (M) on 1 June 1843 and died at Chattanooga, Tenn. on 14 March 1933. He was the son of Edwin (b. 8 Sept 1818; d. 16 Dec 1902) and Mary C. (b.24 July 1820; d. 21 Dec 1901) Jenness.

Martha Brown was probably born on the farm called *Stellock* in Glasserton Parish where her family resided in 1851 (SC). She was living with the family on *Cairndoon* in the same parish in 1861 (SC). When the family emigrated to this country in 1870, she appears on the passenger list as *Martha Brown, age 17, spinster* (PL). Shortly thereafter she appears in the census enumeration of the family in Hampton Falls, N.H. (USC).

74

The Brown Families

We know little about the early life of Samuel Alonzo Jenness. In 1875 when he married he was a farmer living in North Hampton aged 31 (M). His bride, Martha Brown, was 21 and a resident of the same town (M). In 1880 they appear in the census records of North Hampton with their first two children, living in the same house as his parents:

```
Edwin       Jenness   head   61   farmer          b.  N.H.
Mary E.        "      wife   59   housekeeper         "
Alonzo S.      "      head   37   farmer              "
Martha B.      "      wife   27   housekeeper  b.  Scotland
George W.      "      son     4   -           b.  N.H.
Florence M.    "      dau     2   -               "
```

On 15 Dec 1880 Samuel A. Jenness petitioned the Probate Court at Exeter, N.H. to be appointed guardian to his minor children, George W. Jenness and Florence M. Jenness of North Hampton, N.H. This petition was granted and a bond was drawn up with him as principal, and his parents, Edwin and Mary C. Jenness of North Hampton, as sureties. His wife, Martha B. Jenness witnessed the signatures on the bond. This action was apparently taken because the minor children had received bequests from someone's estate.

The four children of Samuel Alonzo and Martha (Brown) Jenness were all born in North Hampton, N.H. (B), and they were still residing there in 1900 when their son George W. Jenness married (M), so it seems probable that they resided there continuously throughout that period. However, they subsequently removed to Greenland, N.H. where they were living in 1909 when their daughter Clara married (M). In 1916 they were living on Maple Avenue in Greenland (DIR). About 1920 they removed to Amesbury, Mass. where they lived at 115 Congress Street.

Although Martha B. Jenness died before her husband, she left a will dated 10 Aug 1922 in which she bequeathed to her husband Samuel A. Jenness *the use of all my real estate...during his natural life, then to my dauther Florence M. Tyler...* (P). All her personal property not otherwise provided for was also bequeathed to Samuel and daughter Florence with the condition *she coming for and providing a home for said husband* (P). Other heirs mentioned were daughter Clara E. Berry, son Newell C. Jenness, son George W. Jenness, grandson Lester Jenness Tyler, and granddaughter Hazel O. Jenness (P). John P. Titcomb of Amesbury, Mass. was named executor (P). Her estate included a house and barn on a two acre lot at 115 Congress Street in Amesbury, a six acre lot of stump land on Back River in Amesbury, and an eleven acre lot of pasture and field also on Back River (P). The will was proved on 27 Nov 1922 (P).

The Brown Families

Following the death of his wife, Samuel A. Jenness removed to Chattanooga, Tenn. where he resided with his daughter Florence Tyler until his death in 1933.

JENNESS children:

George W. - b. 9 Nov 1875 at North Hampton, N.H. (B).

Florence May - b. 6 Jan 1878 at North Hampton, N.H. (B).

Newell C. - b. 7 June 1880 at North Hampton, N.H. (B).

Clara Elizabeth - b. 24 May 1883 at North Hampton, N.H. (B).

#+#+#+#+#+#+#+#+#+#+#+#+#+#+#+#+#

MARY ANN BROWN was born in Ireland (SC) on 29 July 1846 and died in Hampton Falls, N.H. on 27 June 1924 (D). She was the daughter of William and Isabella (Kennedy) Brown (D). She married Joseph Drysdale, Jr. in Scotland on 7 Dec 1866. He was born in Kirkinner Parish, Wigtonshire, Scotland (SC) on 7 May 1846 (D), the son of Joseph Drysdale, Sr. and his wife Mary (SC). Joseph Drysdale, Jr. died at Hampton Falls, N.H. on 7 March 1924 (D). On his death record his mother's name is given as Mary McClellon (D).

Mary Ann Brown moved from Ireland to Scotland with her parents sometime between 1846 and 1849 as can be deduced from the birth places of her brothers and sisters in the Scottish census records. In 1851 she was residing with her parents on the farm called *Stellock* in Glasserton Parish, Wigtonshire, Scotland at age 8 (SC). A decade later she was living with her parents on *Cairndoon* in the same parish (SC).

Joseph Drysdale, Sr. and his wife Mary were both born in Ireland, but all of their children (except perhaps their eldest child, Ann) were born in Scotland (SC). In 1851 we find the family enumerated in Kirkinner Parish where they were residing in the laborer's house on *Chirnfield*:

Joseph Drysdale	head	36	ag. laborer	b. Ireland
Mary	"	wife	38	embroidery	"
Ann	"	dau	11	-	"
William	"	son	8	scholar	b. Kirkinner
Mary	"	dau	6	-	"
Joseph	"	son	3	-	"
John A.	"	"	1	-	"

76

The Brown Families

A decade later the family resided in Caulside Cottage in Sorbie Parish where they were listed as follows:

Joseph Drysdale	head	45	ag. laborer	b. Ireland		
Mary	"	wife	47	—		"
Ann	"	dau	21	—	b. Kirkinner	
Wm.	"	son	18	ag. laborer	"	
Mary	"	dau	15	—	"	
Joseph	"	son	13	scholar	"	
John	"	"	11	"	"	
Margaret	"	dau	9	"	b. Sorbie	
Elizabeth	"	"	6	—	"	
Thomas	"	son	3	—	"	

In 1871 the elder Joseph Drysdale was living in the village of Port William in Mochrum Parish with his remaining family:

Joseph Drysdale	head	57	ag. laborer	b. Ireland	
Mary	"	wife	54		"
Annie	"	dau	30	ag. labor	b. Kirkinner
Thomas	"	son	14	scholar	b. Sorbie
Catherine	"	gdau	6	"	b. England
James Wilson	border	23	ag. laborer	b. Inch	

Joseph Drysdale, Jr. is said to have married Mary Ann Brown in 1866. In 1871 we find them also living in Port William Village with a small family:

Joseph Drysdale	head	22	ag. labor	b. Kirkinner	
Mary A.	"	wife	27	—	b. Ireland
William	"	son	3	—	b. Glasserton
Mary	"	dau	1	—	"

Later in 1871 Joseph Drysdale brought his family to America. They arrived in Boston, Mass. on the steamship *Tarifa* on 24 April 1871 after a passage from Liverpool in steerage class (PL). They appear on the passenger list as follows:

Jos. Drysdale	28	laborer
Mary	"	27	—
Wm.	"	1	—
Mary	"	27	spinster

The ages of the children are grossly in error. They took up residence in Hampton Falls, N.H. where we find the family in the 1880 census:

The Brown Families

Joseph Drysdale	head	32	shoemaker	b. Scotland
Mary A.	"	wife	–	housekeeper	"
Wm.	"	son	13	school	"
Mary	"	dau	9	–	"
Martha	"	"	7	–	b. N.H.
Maggie	"	"	5	–	"
John	"	son	3	–	"

The home occupied by the Drysdale family in Hampton Falls had formerly stood near Lewis F. Prescott's, and was there occupied by Mrs. Sally (Melcher) Sanborn (HF). It was moved to the site where the Drysdale's occupied it in 1875 (HF). By a deed dated 14 June 1883 Joseph Drysdale of Hampton Falls, purchased and acre of land in that town from John C. Akerman for $133 (DD). He bought a three acre field there on 1 Oct 1885 from Abigail A. Green of that town for $210 (DD). In an undated deed, which was acknowledged on 29 July 1901, Edwin Janvrin of Hampton Falls conveyed about one acre of tillage land there to Joseph Drysdale of that town for $1 (DD). The latter property was bounded on the north by the homestead of Joseph Drysdale and on the east by Old Post Road (DD).

In 1891 when his daughter Mary married, Joseph Drysdale was described as a shoemaker as he had been also in the 1880 census (M). In 1916 he and wife Mary Ann were residing on the Hampton Road in Hampton Falls, and he was described as a stonemason, an occupation also mentioned in the following obituary from the *Exeter News-Letter* of 7 March 1924:

> *HAMPTON FALLS - On Saturday, March 8, Joseph Drysdale died at his home here. Although his health had been failing for many months, the end came suddenly. Mr. Drysdale was born in Scotland, but came to this country when a young man. He married Mary, daughter of the late William Brown, about sixty years ago and settled in Hampton Falls. She survives him, as do five of their six children: Mrs. Rowe of Newburyport; Mrs. Clark of this town; Mrs. Evan of Derry; William of North Hampton, and John of Haverhill, Mass. Mr. Drysdale was a stonemason by trade and was considered a fine workman. He was an honest, industrious citizen, respected by all who knew him.*

Following the death of the widow, Mary Ann (Brown) Drysdale, in 1924, the following obituary appeared in the Exeter News-Letter of July 4th:

> *Mary, widow of Joseph Drysdale died at her home on the Lafayette Road last Friday. She was born in Scotland, the daughter of the late William Brown, and was about*

*eighty years old. She came to Hampton Falls in the late
60's and has been a highly respected citizen. She leaves
beside her five children, three brothers, John, William, and
Andrew Brown. This is the 4th death in the neighborhood
this year. Mr. Drysdale passed away last March.*

DRYSDALE children:

William - b. Glasserton Parish, Wigtonshire, Scotland (SC)
    on 9 Dec 1867 (D).
Mary M. - b. Glasserton Parish on 3 May 1870 (D).

Martha B. - b. Hampton Falls, N.H. on 7 July 1874 (D).

Margaret D. - b. Hampton Falls, N.H. on 7 Dec 1875 (D).

John - b. Hampton Falls, N.H. on 7 May 1878 (D).

Annie F. - b. Hampton Falls, N.H. on 7 Sept 1887 (D).

#+#+#+#+#+#+#+#+#+#+#+#+#+#+#

MAUDE AILEEN BROWN was born Hampton, N.H. on 23
July 1888, daughter of Jonathan O. and Carrie Perkins (P).
Following the death of her mother she was cared for and subsequently adopted by John and Mary P. (Tarleton) Brown (P).
Maude A. Brown was a member of the Class of 1908 at the
Robinson Female Seminary in Exeter. She traveled to and from
school each day over the electic car tracks which John Brown
had helped construct. As a young woman she worked as a
seamstress in various homes for $1 per day. Following the
death of her parents she worked for two years for Dr. Wm.
Coleman of Seabrook, N.H., their family physician. The next
twenty years she was a housekeeper/companion to Miss Amy E.
Ware, a teacher in State Teacher's College in Salem, Mass.
During this period she lived in Marblehead, Mass. In 1962 she
took up residence at the Eventide Home in Exeter, N.H. where
she passed the time reading current events and crocheting. Miss
Brown had a keen interest in this genealogy and provided the
compilers with a wealth of information regarding the early generations. She died at the Eventide Home 31 December 1978. Her
ancestry is given in Dow's History of Hampton, N.H. 2/916.

#+#+#+#+#+#+#+#+#+#+#+#+#+#+#

MORRILL HOWARD BROWN was born at Exeter, N.H. on
29 November 1903, the son of George C. and May (Lee) Brown.
On 13 July 1935 he married Elva Lillian Hersey at Wolfeboro,

N.H. She was born at Tuftonboro, N.H. on 19 January 1915, the daughter of Edwin Charles and Hattie Belle (Springer) Hersey. She attended Brewster Academy at Wolfeboro, N.H. in the class of 1933. Mr. Brown worked for many years as a truck driver. They resided in Tuftonborough, N.H. for many years.

BROWN children:

SHIRLEY ANN – b. Wolfeboro, N.H. on 7 March 1936.

PRISCILLA MAY – b. Wolfeboro, N.H. on 23 November 1938.

JAMES HOWARD – b. Wolfeboro, N.H. on 21 May 1945.

#+#+#+#+#+#+#+#+#+#+#+#+#+#+#

LAWRENCE GEORGE BROWN was born at Exeter, N.H. on 7 June 1906, the son of George C. and May (Lee) Brown. He died in Exeter, N.H. on 18 May 1963 unmarried.

For many years Lawrence George Brown, or "Lorny" as he was widely known, operated a jewelry and watch repair shop in the Seward Block on Water Street in Exeter. When he died in 1963 he was employed by the Wise Shoe Company in Exeter. He was survived by: two sisters, Mrs. Myrle Bristol of Milford, and Mrs. Mahlon Clough of Portsmouth; a brother, Morrill Brown of Wolfeboro and several nieces and nephews. Bearers were Clyde Maxwell, Fred Maxwell, Hugh MacDougal, John Poggio, John MacGregor, and Henry Watson. He is buried in the family lot in the Exeter Cemetery where the iscription reads:

Lawrence G. Brown b. 1906 d. 1963

#+#+#+#+#+#+#+#+#+#+#+#+#+#+#

NANCY MERROW BROWN was born at Haverhill, Mass. on 22 Jan 1957, the daughter of Bremner Howard and Marcia Merrow (McCarthy) Brown. She has been a Brownie and Girl Scout, and has studied piano and ballet. She also enjoys skiing and swimming. She is a graduate of Wheaton College.

#+#+#+#+#+#+#+#+#+#+#+#+#+#+#

NILE HOLMES BROWN was born at Odiorne's Point at Rye Beach, N.H. on 15 October 1894, the son of Andrew G. and Nora V. (Holmes) Brown. He died at Central Falls, R.I. on 10 August 1957. He married (1) Laura I. Bousquet at Somersworth, N.H. on 18 May 1912. She was born in Canada about 1890, the daughter of Andrew and Edvige (Daignault) Bousquet. They resided in

Louise (DeLong) Brown, Nile H. Brown, & Vivian D. Brown
Bernice Arlene Brown (front)

Nile Holmes Brown, Jr. (rear)
Carl G., Addison O. & Joyce A. Brown

Bernice A., Nile H., Jr., & Vivian D. Brown

Worcester, Mass. about 1914. She was a very pretty actress. They divorced shortly thereafter without issue. He married (2) Emily Louise DeLong in New York City in 1919. She was born in Houlton, Me. on 4 July 1899.

The house where Nile Holmes Brown was born on Odiorne's Point subsequently became part of the U.S. Government Military Reservation which is now a State Park. As a boy he lived with his parents on the Parson's Farm at Rye Beach. There he had a goat which pulled a small cart, and he played along the ocean shoreline with his older sister. He was attending grade school in Exeter in 1907 (DIR) after his parents had separated.

During most of his life Mr. Brown earned his livelihood at the mechanical arts. At various times he was employed as a tool and die maker, as an auto mechanic, and as a general maintenence man. Later in life he lived principally around Bridgeport, Conn. and Central Falls, R.I. Mr. Brown served briefly with the Engineers during WWI being stationed at Ft. Devens. He is buried in the family plot in the North Side Cemetery on Garland Rd., Nottingham, N.H. near the home where his parents lived as newlyweds.

The widow Emily Louise (DeLong) Brown married (2) on 12 May 1973 Mr. Harry Pike at South Attleboro, Mass. He died 13 March 1978 and was buried in Hodgdon Cemetery.

BROWN children:

MARJORIE LOUISE - b. Bridgeport, Conn. on 18 September 1919.
BERNICE ARLENE - b. Worcester, Mass. on 20 April 1921.

NILE HOLMES - b. Bridgeport, Conn. on 13 January 1925.

VIVIAN DeLONG - b. New Haven, Conn. on 6 August 1928.

CARL GARFIELD - b. 13 November 1929; died young.

ADDISON ORLAND - b. Bridgeport, Conn. on 14 March 1933.

JOYCE ADELE - b. Bridgeport, Conn. on 3 January 1936.

#+#+#+#+#+#+#+#+#+#+#+#+#+#

NILE HOLMES BROWN, Jr.,was born in Bridgeport, Conn. on 13 Jan 1925, the son of Nile Holmes and Emily Louise (DeLong) Brown. He married Lorraine Meunier on 5 July 1949 at Pawtucket, R.I. She was born there on 13 Aug 1928, the daughter of William and Medora (Poisson) Peter of Mooseup, Conn.

The Brown Families

Mr. Brown prefers to be called "Jack". As a young man he worked for the New York, New Haven, and Hartford Railroad where he began as a freight handler, but at the time of his induction into the U.S. Air Force on 23 June 1943 he had advanced to baggage master and ticket agent in the Attleboro, Mass. depot. Regarding his military service he says:

> *Half of my time was spent in the U.S.A. the other half in E.T.O. Europe. The highest rank I received was T5 Corporal. I served 18 months in the 568th Anti-Aircraft Battalion but was attached to the 4th Air Force in California. I did basic training at Camp Haan, active duty training was at Camp Irwin in Mojave Desert. After basic training we went to advance training at Camp Shelby, Mississippi, and another camp in Georgia (I can't recall the name). Then to Camp Kilmer, New Jersey, for overseas duty in Europe. On arrival in England I was attached to the Eighth Air Force and also later on to the 9th. Three days after D-Day I arrived in France. At that time U.S. was trying to liberate Paris. After a few days of staying in France in the Black Forest, we left for Belguim. From what I understand we played some part in liberating Belguim. I was stationed at a marshland area when the Battle of the Bulge broke out. At that time I was alerted to a trucking outfit. I drove the red ball until war ended. Did not have enough points to come home so went to a rest camp for two weeks. I did nothing but relax and enjoy myself. Then was assigned my last three months of service to the 12-23rd M.P.S., then was shipped home for discharge. Happy Day!*

Mr. Brown received the Good Conduct Medal, European African Middle Eastern Theatre Campaign Ribbon, American Theatre Campaign Ribbon, and Victory Medal.

The family is very musically inclined; Lorraine plays the piano and organ, and all members of the family have fine singing voices. They enjoy making musical tape cassett recordings which they exchange with other members of the family back home. Jack also has a talent for dancing. While in the sevice at Camp Edwards he performed in service men's shows, and later appeared on stage at other places a few times, including several appearances in Las Vegas. Jack now enjoys gardening and furniture refinishing; Lorry enjoys sewing, knitting, cooking, and gardening. She also works as a check-out clerk in a local grocery store. The family resides in Cypress, California.

BROWN children:

The Brown Families

DAVID NILE - b. Central Falls, R.I. on 28 Feb 1950.

ARLENE BARBARA - b. Attleboro, Mass. on 6 April 1955.

Jeffrey Robert - b. Fullerton, Calif. on 31 July 1959. He
enjoys mechanical things and athletics, especially
wrestling.

#+#+#+#+#+#+#+#+#+#+#+#+#+#+#

NORMAN ROBERT BROWN was born in North Conway, N.H.
on 5 July 1912, the son of Clarence Warren and Thannie W.
(Gleason) Brown. On 1 Jan 1937 he married Kathleen LaCoy at
Portsmouth, N.H. She was born at Concord, N.H. on 5 May 1913,
the daughter of George E. and Katherine J. (Nichols) LaCoy.
Mr. Brown is a gaduate of Colby College and is Past President of the N.H. Hospital Association and the New England
Hospital Assembly. He was Administrator of the Concord Hospital in Concord, N.H. about 1970, and resided there.

BROWN children:

G. GEOFFREY - b. Brooklyn, N.Y. on 7 March 1941.

Jill - b. Brooklyn, N.Y. on 28 March 1946. On 16 Aug 1969
she married Bruce Fuller.
Norman Robert - b. Salem, Mass. on 21 March 1950. He
entered the U.S. Navy in Sept 1969.
Judith A. - b. Concord, N.H. on 4 June 1959.

#+#+#+#+#+#+#+#+#+#+#+#+#+#+#

PRISCILLA MAY BROWN was born at Wolfeboro, N.H. on
23 November 1938, daughter of Morrill Howard and Elva Lillian
(Hersey) Brown. She married Robert Gienty at Manchester, N.H.
on 21 November 1968. He was born at Warner, N.H. on 23
September 1924, the son of F. Kenneth and Jane (Whytock)
Gienty. Mr. Gienty was formerly employed as a truck driver and
custodian. About 1970 the couple lived in Concord, N.H.; they
formerly lived in Phoenix, Arizona. No children.

#+#+#+#+#+#+#+#+#+#+#+#+#+#+#

RICHARD CLARENCE BROWN was born at Portsmouth,
N.H. on 15 Jan 1916, the son of Clarence Warren and Thannie
Wales (Gleason) Brown. He married Margaret Eleanor Mueller
at Buffalo, N.Y. on 14 Feb 1948. She is the daughter of George
E. and Amelia (Kuhnle) Mueller. Mr.Brown was in the 30th

Cavalry in WWII. He served from 25 Nov 1942 to 22 Oct 1945 in Normandy, Northern France, Ardennes, Central Europe, and the Rhineland. About 1970 he was a buyer for the U.S. Air Force and resided with his wife in Nashua, N.H. No children.

#+#+#+#+#+#+#+#+#+#+#+#+#+#+#

ROBERT BROWN was born in Ireland (SC) on 25 Dec 1843, son of William and Isabella (Kennedy) Brown (D). He died in Hampton Falls, N.H. on 25 April 1910 (D). On 12 Nov 1874 Robert Brown was married to Janet Brown at Seabrook, N.H. by Rev. Geo. H. Pratt (M). Janet Brown was born in Glasserton Parish, Wigtonshire, Scotland on 29 Oct 1839, the daughter of William and Margaret (McDowall) Brown (PR). She died in Hampton Falls, N.H. on 20 June 1924 at age 85 (D).

Janet Brown was the oldest of six children found recorded to William and Margaret (McDowall) Brown in the Glasserton Parish register as follows (PR):

> *Janet - b. 29 Oct 1839; bapt. 10 Nov 1839*
> *Joseph - b. 31 May 1842*
> *John - b. 23 Feb. 1846*
> *Sarah - b. 10 Sept 1848; bapt. 15 Oct 1848*
> *Samuel - b. 25 Aug 1850; bapt. 15 Sept 1850*
> *Hugh - b. 20 Sept 1854; bapt. 5 Oct 1854*

Family sources indicate that there was at least one other child, Margaret, and that three sisters, Janet, Sarah, and Margaret all came to Hampton FAlls, N.H. from Scotland. It is probable that some other members of the family also emigrated to the United States, but particulars are lacking.

It appears from the births of his brothers and sisters that Robert Brown moved from Ireland to Scotland with his parents between 1846 and 1849 (SC). In 1851 he was living with his parents on the farm called *Stellock* in Glasserton Parish, Wigtonshire, Scotland where he was a student (SC). A decade later he was a ploughman living in the household of William Smith on the farm called *Craigdhu* in the same parish (SC). His sister Jane was employed as a kitchen maid in the same household (SC).

Robert Brown came to the United States a few years later. According to family tradition he came over with his younger brother, John, but details are lacking (see John Brown). In 1870 after the arrival of his parents he resided in their household in Hampton Falls, N.H., he being employed as a farm laborer (USC). When he married in 1874 he was still a farmer (M).

In 1880 Robert Brown resided in Hampton Falls with his young family where they were enumerated as follows (USC):

The Brown Families

```
Robert Brown    head   40   shoemaker     b. Scotland
Janet      "    wife   39   housekeeper        "
Wm.        "    son    3      -          b. N.H.
```

They shared their dwelling with Robert's sister, Mary Ann and her husband, Joseph Drysdale, and their family (USC).

Robert and Janet Brown later owned a house on Murray's Row, now Lafayette Road, in Hampton Falls which had been moved to that location in 1874 (HF). The house had previously been occupied by Sally Healey and Polly Dow (HF). Robert Brown became a naturalized citizen before the Supreme Court in Exeter, N.H. on 25 April 1890 (N).

At his death in 1910 Robert Brown was again described as a farmer (D). He died intestate, his only heirs being widow Janet and son William (P). The latter was appointed administrator of the estate which was valued at $2300.00 (P). The estate included a 1 acre homestead and ten acres of field and pasture land (P). The following obituary appeared in the *Exeter News-Letter* of 29 April 1910:

> *Mr. Robert Brown died Monday afternoon at his home in Hampton Falls in his 67th year. He was born in Scotland, whence in 1872 he came with his parents and brothers to Hampton Falls. There he had since lived, a useful citizen. He leaves a widow, a son, William, and three brothers, Andrew, John, and William H. Brown, all of Hampton Falls. The funeral was on Wednesday afternoon, conducted by Rev. Charles A. Parker of the Baptist Church in Hampton Falls.*

The statements about his being born in Scotland and coming to Hampton Falls in 1872 are both in error.

The widow Janet Brown remained in Hampton Falls. She was living in a house on Hampton Road there about 1916 (DIR), and appears to have lived there until her death in 1924 (D). She left no estate (P). The following obituary appeared in the *Exeter News-Letter* of 4 July 1924:

> *HAMPTON FALLS - On the 19th occurred the death of Jeanette, widow of Robert Brown, at her home here. She was one of our oldest residents, being 84 years old. She was born in Scotland, but lived here about 50 years. She leaves to mourn her loss, a sister, Mrs John Cannon, and in Hampton, a son, William Brown, three grand children and one great grand child. Funeral services were held the following Sunday afternoon and burial was in the village churchyard.*

The Brown Families

Robert and Janet Brown are buried in the cemetery near the Baptist Church at the square in Hampton Falls. The son buried there is said by family sources to have been the first born, and to have died as an infant. The inscriptions read:

```
Robert Brown b. 25 Dec 1844 d. 25 April 1910
Janet Brown b. 7 Jan 1838 d. 20 June 1924
Robert, son of Robert and Janet Brown., 1878
```

BROWN children:

WILLIAM - b. Hampton Falls, N.H. on 2 Aug 1876 (D).

Robert - died as infant, 1878.

#+#+#+#+#+#+#+#+#+#+#+#+#+#

ROBERT BROWN was born in Glasserton Parish, Wigton-shire, Scotland (SC) on 6 July 1861 (FR). He was the son of Benjamin B. and Elizabeth (Thompson) Brown (D). He died in Amesbury, Mass. on 8 Aug 1909 (D) and is buried there in Union Cemetery (C). On 25 Nov 1880 he married (1) Ida A. Winn at Stratham, N.H. (M). She was born at Tuftonborough, N.H. (M) on 12 March 1863. She was the daughter of Jacob Winn (M). After the birth of their only child, Robert and Ida were divorced. Robert married (2) Isabelle Wiseman from Scotland. They had no issue and Isabelle returned to Scotland after Robert's death. Ida (Winn) Brown married as her second husband Bernard Dougherty. She died at Portsmouth, N.H. on 15 July 1931 and is buried in Greenland, N.H.

Robert Brown was living as an infant with his parents on the farm called *Knock* in Glasserton Parish, Wigtonshire, Scotland in 1861 (SC). A decade later at age ten he was still there and was employed as a part-time farm worker (SC). He came to the United States with his parents on the steamship *Olympus*, arriving in Boston, Mass. on 18 April 1872 (PL). According to family tradition he was severely seasick on the passage over and would have jumped over-board, if the family members had not restrained him. The family took up residence in Brentwood, N.H. shortly after arriving in the United States and Robert Brown apparently lived there with them for several years.

In mid-1880 Robert Brown was boarding in the household of William Wentworth in Stratham, N.H., and he was then employed in a machine shop (USC). In November of that year when he married Ida A. Winn, he was a resident of Brentwood, N.H. and was employed as a brass finisher (M). They were married by John S. Batchelder, Clegyman of Stratham, N.H. (M). It was the first marriage for both of them (M). Robert and Ida appear to

Robert L. & Isabelle (Wiseman) Brown
Clarence W. Brown (child)

have been living in Greenland, N.H. in 1883 when their only child was born. In 1909 when he died Robert Brown was living at 13 Union St. in Amesbury, Mass., and was a woodworker (D).

The following obituary appeared in the *Exeter News-Letter* of 20 Aug 1909:

> *Brentwood - Mr. and Mrs. B.B. Brown have been bereft of their son, Robert L. Brown, who passed away at his recent home on Union Street in Amesbury, Mass. on the evening of Sunday the 8th instant.*
>
> *Robert Brown was but a litte over 48 years of age at the time of his departure from this life. He had been a sufferer for some time of tuberculosis.*
>
> *The deceased was a native of Brentwood and at one time was engaged in the shoe-making business in this town. He left home at the age of fifteen years for Newburyport, Mass., where he found employment with a gentleman named Dockham at farming. A few years later he went to Stratham where he took up farming and gardening. He was married in Stratham. From Stratham he removed to Amesbury, and being a born mechanic, he quickly learned the business of auto body-building in which he was engaged until his last illness enfeebled him. He was not identified with any society or church, but was a positive believer in Christianity. He was a quiet, peaceful, law abiding citizen and in sickness he was uncomplaining. Besides his aged parents he leaves a widow and a son, five brothers and three sisters.*

According to family tradition Robert Brown adopted the middle name Livermore. That is consistent with the initial given in his obituary, but his death record, for which his wife Isabelle was the informant, clearly shows the middle initial "S". The statement in the obituary that he was a native of Brentwood is clearly in error. He is buried in Lot No. 102 in Union Cemetery in Amesbury, Mass.

BROWN child:

CLARENCE WARREN - b. Greenland, N.H. on 19 March 1883.

#+#+#+#+#+#+#+#+#+#+#+#+#+#

ROBERT ORLANDO BROWN was born in Hampton, N.H. on 28 August 1898, the son of William and Cora E. (Blake) Brown. On 3 November 1921 he married Helen Mae Kimball at Lawrence, Mass. She was born there on 3 January 1898, the daughter of Daniel W. and Sarah Rebecca (Brooks) Kimball.

The Brown Families

Mr. Brown worked for many years as a custodian, but had retired by 1971 and lived on Mill Road in Hampton, N.H. with his wife. Mrs. Brown taught school at Hampton Academy for 28 years and then worked as a typist at the Tobey and Merrill Insurance Company for six years.

Mr. Brown died 12 July 1978 leaving, in adition to his wife, two daughters, Mrs. Betty J. Blatchford, Hampton and Mrs. Shirley A. Carter, North Hampton; a sister, Mrs. Hazel B. Coffin, Hampton; a brother, Clyde W. Brown, Raymond; seven grandchildren, two great grandchildren, several nieces and nephews. He was buried in High Stret Cemetery, the bearers being Earl Blatchford, Harlan E. Carter, Paul T. Carter, Harlan E. Carter, Jr., Lester B. Tobey and Pieter Fink.

BROWN children:

BETTY JANE - b. Exeter, N.H. on 2 March 1924.

SHIRLEY ANN - b. Portsmouth, N.H. on 9 May 1927.

#+#+#+#+#+#+#+#+#+#+#+#+#+#+#+#

SHIRLEY ANN BROWN was born in Portsmouth, N.H. on 9 May 1927, the daughter of Robert O. and Helen Mae (Kimball) Brown. She graduated from Hampton Academy and High School, and then entered the University of New Hampshire from which she graduated with a B.A. degree in Psychology. She has taught in the Hampton area schools for several years, and was the North Hampton correspondent for the *Hampton Union*.

On 19 February 1946 she married Harlan Edward Carter at Hampton, N.H. He was born at North Hampton, N.H. on 7 July 1926, the son of Harry E. and Nellie (Marston) Carter. Mr. Carter graduated from Hampton Academy and High School and served in the U.S. Air Force 1945-1946. He is a mason.

CARTER children:

Paul Terry - b. Exeter, N.H. on 4 October 1946.

Sonja Lee - b. Exeter, N.H. on 22 November 1947.

Harlan Edward - b. Exeter, N.H. on 25 October 1951.

Beverly Ann - b. Exeter, N.H. on 31 August 1954.

Robert Harry - b. Exeter, N.H. on 20 December 1957.

Sherri Lyn - b. Exeter, N.H. on 29 December 1963

The Brown Families

SHIRLEY ANN BROWN was born in Wolfeboro, N.H. on 7 March 1936, the daughter of Morrill Howard and Elva Lillian (Hersey) Brown. She received her education at Brewster Academy and Plymouth State College in N.H. She taught elementary school in Portsmouth, N.H. and Springfield, Mass. for six years. She has served as Assistant Sunday School Superintendent at the Federated Church of Chicopee, Mass.

On 4 July 1964 she married Leslie Hamilton Coulter at the Community Church of Melvin Village, N.H. He was born on 6 August 1911, the son of James and Edith (Jenkinson) Coulter of County Armagh, Northern Ireland.

Mr. Coulter was an airplane mechanic in the U.S. Army Air Force during WWII in Texas, and is now employed by the American Saw and Mfg. Co. in East Longmeadow, Mass. The family resides in Chicopee, Mass.

COULTER children:

Kevin James – b. Springfield, Mass. on 2 January 1965.

Jeffrey Alan – b. Springfield, Mass. on 14 June 1966.

Amy Lynn – b. Springfield, Mass. on 22 December 1968.

#+#+#+#+#+#+#+#+#+#+#+#+#+#

VIVIAN DELONG BROWN was born at New Haven, Conn. on 6 Aug 1928, the daughter of Nile Holmes and Emily Louise (DeLong) Brown. As a young woman she sang in a trio known as "The Brown Sisters" with her sisters, Marjorie and Bernice. She married (1) Charles Clyden Argabright; they had three children. She married (2) Johnnie S. Clark. They have a daughter and resided in Memphis, Tenn. about 1970.

ARGABRIGHT children:

Sharon Emerald –

Charlene DeLong –

Glen Clyden –

CLARK child:

Dawn –

#+#+#+#+#+#+#+#+#+#+#+#+#+#

The Brown Families

WILLIAM BROWN was born in Ireland (SC) on 11 Aug 1819, the son of William and Martha (McLimon) Brown (D). He died in Hampton Falls, N.H. on 12 Feb 1908 (D). William Brown married Isabella Kennedy in County Down, Ireland in December of 1835 (B-dau Isabella). She was born in Ireland about 1820 (SC) and died in Hampton Falls on 21 May 1894 (D).

Like millions of others William Brown fled from Ireland with his family during the Great Potato Famine. The exact date of their emigration has not been determined, but it is evident from the births of the children that they made the move between the years 1846-1849 (SC). Many of these refugees settled as itinerant laborers in Scotland which is where we first find the family in official records. In the census of 1851 William Brown and his family were living and working on a farm by the name of *Stellock* in Glasserton parish, Wigtonshire, Scotland. The family was enumerated as follows (SC):

```
William Brown   head   34  ag. lab.   b. Ireland
Isabella    "   wife   34   -                "
Isabella    "   wife   34   -                "
Benjamin    "   son    14  farm lab.         "
Jane        "   dau    12   -                "
Robert      "   son    10  scholar          "
Maryann     "   dau     8   -                "
John        "   son     3   -          b. Glasserton,
                                          Wigtonshire
```

The family next appears in the 1861 census living on the neighboring farm called *Cairndoon* where they were enumerated as follows (SC):

```
William Brown   head   41  ag. lab.   b. Ireland
Isabella    "   wife   41   -                "
Maryann     "   dau    15   -                "
John        "   son    12  scholar   b. Glasserton
Martha      "   dau     9   -                "
William     "   son     4   -                "
Andrew      "   son     2   -                "
Alexander Brodey -      1  boarder           "
```

The farms *Stellock* and *Cairndoon* are large coastal farms situated on bluffs over-looking the Bay of Luce. In 1970 they were still known by those names and were still being worked.

At about the age of fifty William Brown emigrated to the United States with his wife and four youngest children, following his sons Robert and John who had come over in 1868 or 1869. The family came steerage from Liverpool, England on the

90

The Brown Families

steamship *Palmyra*, arriving in Boston Mass. on 18 April 1870. They appear on the ship's passenger list as follows (PL):

```
Wm.       Brown   50 laborer
Isabell    "      45    -
Martha     "      17 spinster
Wm.        "      13 laborer
Andrew     "       9    -
Isabell    "       6    -
```

William Brown's married daughter, Jane, and her husband, William Whenal also came on that ship with several of their children (PL). Only William Brown's oldest son, Benjamin, and his married daughter, Mary Ann, remained in Scotland, but they would soon emigrate also.

The Brown and Whenal families arrived in the United States in time to be enumerated in the 1870 census where we find the two families sharing a house in Hampton Falls, N.H. (USC). The Brown family appears in that census as follows (USC):

```
William Brown   48 farm laborer   b. Ireland
Isabella   "    48 housekeeper        "
Robert     "    24 farm laborer   b. Scotland
John       "    21  "       "         "
Martha     "    17 dom. servant       "
William    "    14 shoe factory       "
Andrew     "    12 school             "
Isabella   "     7  "                 "
```

That census also reveals that there were several other families of Scotch-Irish background living in Hampton Falls at that time, but we know nothing to connect them with this Brown family.

By 1880 several more of the children had married and left home. In the census of that year for Hampton Falls the family of William Brown was enumerated as follows (USC):

```
William Brown   head   57 farmer      b. Scotland
Bella K.   "    wife   57 housekeeper     "
Wm.        "    son    24 shoemaker       "
Andrew     "    son    21    "            "
```

This as well as most subsequent records pertaining to William Brown or his family indicate that he was born in Scotland. However, it is clear from the Scottish census records that he was born in Ireland, although he sojourned in Scotland for over twenty years.

The Brown Families

The homestead occupied by William Brown and his family in Hampton Falls has an interesting history. It was originally built by William A. Hopkins, an Englishman who came to Hampton Falls about 1848 (HF). He is said to have dug hundreds of miles of drainage ditches in the salt marshes to make it possible to harvest the salt hay that grew there (HF). After his death the property passed to John H. and Sarah Gove of Hampton Falls who sold the property to Robert and John Brown, also of Hampton Falls, for $825.00 by a deed dated 5 Dec 1872 (DD).

The property consisted of *a certain tract of land with building thereon situate in Hampton Falls, containing two acres, more or less, being the homestead of the late Wm. A. Hopkins...* (DD). The property was bounded on the north by land belonging to the estate of George N. Dodge, westerly by land of J.W. Green, southerly by land of J.M. Marshall and Hans Hamilton, and on the east by the Old Post Road (DD). Also conveyed was a piece of marsh land containing three acres bounded on the north by land of James Creighton, east by J. Poor, south by land of John C. Sanborn, and westerly by land belonging to the heirs of Hannah P. Silsby (DD). In connection with the later parcel the Goves reserved *a priviledge previously granted to a few persons to dig salt mud to a limited extent* (DD).

The Robert and John Brown mentioned in that deed were the sons of William and Isabella (Kennedy) Brown. Two days later on 7 Dec 1872 they conveyed all of the above property to William and Isabella Brown *for and during their natural lives* for $500.00 by a deed of that date (DD). Under the terms of that deed the property would revert to Robert and John Brown following the death of their parents. However, on 11 Oct 1886 they conveyed to their brother, Andrew Brown, of Hampton Falls about one acre of this land on the northern end including the house thereon for $1 (DD). It was thus arranged that the homestead would pass down to Andrew Brown who lived with, and cared for William and Isabella during their declining years.

William and Isabella Brown had an interesting habit observed and related by Clyde Lind (Brown) Buzzell. It seems that back before the turn of the century William and Isabella visited at the Parson Farm in Rye, N.H. with their grandson, Andrew G. Brown, and his family. Andrew's daughter, Clyde, was understandably impressed when she saw the elderly couple step out to the stone wall first thing in the morning before breakfast, find a comfortable perch, and proceed to fill and light their pipes for a pleasant smoke! According to the story Isabella first filled and lighted William's pipe and then her own. These were clay pipes with short, stubby stems of the type we now associate with St. Patrick's Day.

The death of William Brown is recorded in Warren Brown's Journal with the remark that he has been a resident of Hampton

The Brown Families

Falls since 1870 (HF). William Brown died intestate and there was no estate to be administered; the probate file contains only a copy of his death certificate (P). The following death notice and obituary appeared in the *Exeter News-Letter* of 21 Feb 1908:

> *BROWN - In Hampton Falls, February 12, William Brown, aged 88 years, 6 months, 1 day, the town's oldest citizen.*

> *HAMPTON FALLS, February 19 - William Brown, one of Hampton Falls' oldest citizens, passed away at the home of his son, Andrew Brown, Wednesday evening. For 89 years he has been permitted to watch development and progress of the world, but his call came at last and he had to pass through that gate by which all men shall leave this world. He was born in Scotand in 1819 and lived there for 50 years. He was married at the age of 17 and became a contractor, working for many years constructing canals. In 1870 he came to America, where he engaged in farming. His family was large, being composed of six sons and four daughters. Five sons are now living, Benjamin, Robert, John, William and Andrew, all of whom are good, upright men and worthy citizens. Three daughters are still living, married and doing well. He has 34 grandchildren living, 54 great grandchildren and two great great grandchildren, making five generations at the time of his death. Thus he has many to mourn his loss. His wife passed away 14 years ago and since then he has lived with his son Andrew, in whose home he received all that love and kindness could provide for him.*

The statements in the obituary that William Brown was born in Scotland and lived there for fifty years are both undoubtedly in error for the reasons already given. In addition it is exceedingly doubtful that he was engaged in constructing canals; there are no canals in the part of Scotland where he is known to have lived. It is possible that he was so employed in Ireland. However, it is not likely that a man of his humble circumstances could have been a contractor.

There is a family tradition that he worked for many years digging drainage ditches to make marsh land arable; Maude A. Brown has described for us the special deep, narrow shovel used for that purpose. All the records we have found give his occupation as agricultural laborer or farmer. The tradition may be derived from the occupation of the former owner of his house in Hampton Falls who was a digger of drainage ditches in the marshes as noted above.

The Brown Families

William and Isabella (Kennedy) Brown are buried in a family plot in Brookside Cemetery in Hampton Falls, N.H. where the inscriptions read:

```
William Brown, d. 12 Feb 1908 ae. 88y 6m 1d.
Isabella, wife of William Brown, d. 21 June 1894
               ae. 74y 4m.
```

BROWN children:

BENJAMIN B. – b. Ireland (SC) on May 3 1837 (FR).

JANE – b. Ireland (SC) on 15 June 1839 (D).

ROBERT – b. Ireland (SC) on 25 Dec 1843 (D).

MARY ANN – b. Ireland (SC) on 29 July 1846 (D).

JOHN – b. Glasserton parish, Wigtonshire, Scotland (SC) on 27 July 1849.

Andrew – b. Glasserton parish, Wigtonshire, Scotland on 22 April 1851 and baptized there on 26 June 1851 (PR); he died prior to 16 June 1859 when the 2nd Andrew was born; referred to by the family as "Little Andrew".

MARTHA – b. Glasserton parish, Wigtonshire, Scotland on 9 Dec 1852 (PR).

WILLIAM H. – b. on the farm called *Cairndoon* in Glasserton parish, Wigtonshire, Scotland on 4 Feb 1856 (B).

ANDREW C. – b. Glasserton parish, Wigtonshire, Scotland (SC) on 16 June 1859 (C).

ISABELLA – b. Glasserton parish, Wigtonshire, Scotland on 3 May 1863 (B).

#+#+#+#+#+#+#+#+#+#+#+#+#+#+#

WILLIAM BROWN was born on the farm called *Morrach*, Whithorn Parish, Wigtonshire, Scotland on 30 Jan 1859, the son of Benjamin B. and Elizabeth (Thompson) Brown (B). He died unmarried on 31 Oct.____ .

In 1861 William Brown was living on the farm called *Knock* in Glasserton parish, Wigtonshire (SC). A decade later at the age of 12 he was an agricultural laborer on that farm where the family still resided (SC). He came to America with his family on the steamship *Olympus*, arriving in Boston, Mass. on 18 April 1872 (PL). In 1880 he lived at home with his parents in Brentwood, N.H. where he was a teamster at the County Farm (USC). The obituaries of his parents indicate that he was a resident of Auburn, Me. in 1918 and 1919. Family sources indicate that he operated a dry cleaning firm there. The following obituary appeared in the *Exeter News-Letter* (date-unknown) under dateline Brentwood:

> *The body of William Brown who passed away at Amesbury, Mass., on October 31, was brought here for burial in the Center Cemetery, following funeral services in the town Saturday afternoon. He is survived by three brothers, John D. and Andrew G. Brown, both of Amesbury, Mass., and Benjamin Brown of Haverhill, Mass.; three sisters, Mrs. Isabelle Bartlett, of this town, Mrs. Elizabeth Shipley, of Merrimac, Mass., and Mrs. William Sweetland, of Exeter; also several nieces and nephews.*

Although the obituary states that he is buried in the family lot in Brentwood, there is no headstone. He never married.

#+#+#+#+#+#+#+#+#+#+#+#+#+#+#

WILLIAM BROWN was born in Hampton Falls, N.H. on 2 August 1876 (D). He was the son of Robert Brown and his wife Janet (D). He died at Hampton, N.H. on 4 August 1951 and is buried there in High St. Cemetery (D). On 20 May 1898 he married Cora E. Blake at North Hampton, N.H. (M). She was the daughter of Orlando J. Blake, farmer, of Hampton, N.H. and his wife Melinda J. _____. She died there on 9 August 1969 at age 89 and is buried in High St. Cemetery in Hampton (O).

William Brown was living in Hampton Falls, N.H. with his parents in 1880 (USC). He was educated at Hampton Academy (HRC). He still resided in Hampton Falls in 1898 when he was married (M). He was then employed as a farmer (M). About 1907 he was residing in North Hampton with his wife and three children (DIR). At that time his occupation was given as clerk (DIR). In 1916 he was living on Highland Ave. in Hampton (DIR). He was then vice president and manager of the E.G. Cole Co. (DIR), a grocery store, of which he was part owner (HRC). He lived in Hampton for the last thirty-eight years of his life (D)

For many years Mr. Brown had operated a funeral home in Hampton. When he died in 1951 Mr. Brown was the Hampton Town Clerk and Tax Collector, positions he had held for about twenty-five years. He was survived by his wife of 54 years, by two sons, Robert O. Brown of Hampton, and Clyde W Brown of Manchester; a daughter, Mrs. Norman Coffin of Hampton; five grandchildren and three great grandchildren. He was buried in the High Street Cemetery in Hampton.

Mrs. Brown continued to live in Hampton until her death in 1969in the Mill Road home where she was born. She was survived by the three children named below. She also is buried in High Street Cemetery where the inscriptions read:

```
William Brown    2 Aug 1876 - 4 Aug 1951
Cora E. Blake   13 Aug 1879 - 9 Aug 1969
```

BROWN children:

ROBERT ORLANDO - b. Hampton, N.H., 28 August 1898.

CLYDE WALLACE - b. Hampton, N.H., 26 August 1899.

CORA HAZEL - b. Hampton, N.H., 3 May 1901.

#+#+#+#+#+#+#+#+#+#+#+#+#+#+#+#

WILLIAM H. BROWN was born on the farm called *Cairndoon* in Glasserton Parish, Wigtonshire, Scotland on 4 Feb 1856, the son of William and Isabella (Kennedy) Brown (B). He died in Hampton Falls, N.H. on 17 May 1926 (P). William H. Brown married (1) Ellen M., daughter of Zebulon and Mary Dow, at North Hampton, N.H. on 23 Aug 1886 (M). She was born 27 March 1849 (C) and died 24 July 1905 at Anna Jacques Hospital, Newburyport, Mass. ae. 56 (ENL). He then married (2) Margaret Smith of Dedham, Mass. on 6 Sept 1906 at Dedham, Mass. (ENL). She died without issue in a Baptist home in Chestnut Hill, Mass. in October 1957.

William H. Brown came to the United States on the steamship *Palmyra* in 1870 with his parents (PL). He was residing at home with his parents in Hampton Falls, N.H. in the censuses of 1870 and 1880, and was employed in a shoe factory (USC). When he first married in 1886 he was a farmer living in Hampton Falls (M). His first wife, Ellen Dow, had inherited a large farm known as the Governor Meshech Weare homestead from her father on his death in 1858 (HF).

This farm was one of five large farms granted by the town of Hampton in 1640 (HF). According to tradition, George Washington spent a night in that house in consultation with Governor Weare in 1775 after he came north to Cambridge, Mass. to assume command of the Continental Army (HF). The barn burned in 1879, but a large house remained which was used by the Browns as a sanitarium for the treatment of nervous diseases (HF). Ellen (Dow) Brown was a trained nurse, having studied at City Hospital in Boston. The opening of the sanitarium was described as follows in the *Exeter News-Letter* of 12 June 1885:

96

The Brown Families

HAMPTON FALLS - We hear that Miss Ella M. Dow, the owner of the President Weare house will soon open her house for certain invalids from Philadelphia. Miss Dow has now become quite celebrated as an adept in the new system of nursing. She has had good fortune to be put in charge of patients of Dr. S. Weare Mitchell and under her care, very great improvement has taken place in several obstinate cases.

Ellen Brown wrote a will dated 8 Nov 1902 which was probated 12 Sept 1905 (P). Her will reads as follows:

Be it known that I, Ellen D. Brown, of Hampton Falls, in the County of Rockingham and State of New Hampshire, do make and publish this my last will and testament as follows:

First: I direct that all my just debts and funeral expenses, and the expense of administering my estate be paid, as by law they must be.

Second: I give and bequeath to my husband, William H. Brown, all live-stock and poultry which I own at the time of my death.

Third: As to all real estate in said Hampton Falls which I own at my death (including my interest in any which I may own in common with any other person), I give and bequeath the same to Mrs. Helen Birtwell of Brookline, Mass., and her heirs and assigns forever, in case she shall, by writing filed in the Probate Office for said County within one year after the grant of letters testimentory or, administration, on my estate, signify her election to accept this device. And if she does not so elect, then I give and bequeath the same to my husband aforesaid, his heirs and assigns forever. But, in either event, whether said real estate goes to my husband or to said Helen Birtwell, the one to whom it does go shall pay to the other a sum equal to one-half the net value of said real estate by which term ("net value"), I mean the total value of my interest (making due reduction of the estimate in case there is any mortgage thereon), less such portion of my debts, funeral charges and administration expenses, as would in the regular course of administration unless the ordinary rules of the law fall upon said real estate, together with said real estate and precisely as if it were a part thereof. I give bequeath and devise to the same person who under the foregoing device takes said real estate all household furniture (in the broadest sense of the term) and all tools and implements of husbandry owned by me at time of my death...the same to be treated as if part and

97

parcel of the real estate shall pay to the one not taking it. And I expressly charge upon said real estate the same under the foregoing provisions the one who does take it is to pay to the one who does not.

Fourth: As to the rest and residue and remainder of my estate, including all that I may own at the time of my decease, whether acquired before or after making this will, I give, bequeath and devise the same to my said husband William H. Brown and the said Helen Birtwell in equal shares, and to their heirs and assigns forever.

Fifth: I hereby appoint said Helen Birtwell sole executrix of this will, and exempt her from giving surety on her bond as such execution, and revoke all former wills.

In construing this will, it is my intention and I direct all my debts (other than mortgage debts), funeral expenses, and expenses of administration, first, upon my personal property, and next (if that be insufficient), upon my real estate, and that such portion of said charges as would by such adjustment fall upon the real estate to be taken into account in estimating the value of the real estate and determining how much the taker of the real estate shall pay to the other beneficiary.

In testimony whereof, I have hereto set my hand this 8th day of November in the year 1902.

Signed: Ellen D. Brown

Witnesses: S. Louisa Huntington, Annie E. Aldrich, and Charles N. Dodge.

This will was presented for probate on 12 Sept 1905 and Helen Birtwell of Brookline, Mass. was appointed executrix. She in turn appointed William H. Brown of Hampton Falls, N.H. to act as her agent (P). Helen Birtwell was apparently a close relation of Ellen Dow as indicated by the following item from the *Exeter News-Letter* of 19 Oct 1894:

BIRTTWELL-DOW - A very lovely home wedding was quietly celebrated at the old Governor Weare place in Hampton Falls, now the residence of Mr. William Brown, on Tuesday noon. Mr. Charles W. Birtwell, Secretary of the Children's Aid Society, of Boston, was then and there married to Miss Helen Dow, also of Boston, but formerly of Hampton Falls. Rev. A. C. Nickerson being the officiating minister. After the usual congratulations, and a delightful feast of good things, Mr. and Mrs. Birtwell left the old homestead to drive to Newburyport, whence they left on their wedding journey.

The Brown Families

The passing of Ellen (Dow) Brown was noted in the *Exeter News-Letter* of 28 July 1905 as follows:

BROWN - At the Anna Jaques Hospital in Newburyport, Mass., July 24, Ellen, wife of William Brown, of Hampton, Falls, N.H., age 56 years.

And elsewhere in the same paper:

Mrs. William Brown of Hampton Falls. - Hampton Falls loses one of its best known and most useful residents in Mrs. Brown, who died on the 24th in Newburyport hospital of pneumonia following acute rheumatism, from which she had suffered for a few weeks. She was clear of mind and conscious of her condition, and that she had well-deserved the medical attendance of Dr. Douglas of Amesbury Dr. Hurd and Dr. Day of Newburyport, and Dr. Jackson of Boston. Her funeral took place at her home, the ancient Weare mansion, on Wednesday afternoon. She is buried beside her father and mother, the Dows, in the nearby cemetery.

Ellen Dow was the daughter of Zebulon and Mary Anne Dow, born in the Weare house in 1849, and grew to womanhood in her native town. Her talent for nursing the sick attracted the notice of the late Dr. C. H. Sanborn and she was employed by him for some time as a nurse. She then trained professionally under Dr. Cowles at the City Hospital in Boston, and returned to the care of patients in Hampton Falls. Her skill and sympathy by her profession came to the knowledge of Dr. Weir Mitchell of Philadelphia, and for more than 25 years he placed his nervous patients under her care - at first in Philadelphia - and then in her own home at Hampton Falls (built 1737), which she modernized after her parents' death, and has become a commodious sanatarium under her direction, and has received and benefited many patients during the years under her direction, since 1880.

She married William Brown who survives her. Mrs Brown was a remarkable woman of character and unusual experiences. She lacked the advantages of early education, but became accomplished in many ways after she took up her profession and made herself one of the most skilled and successful nurses, and was besides, of great benevolence, energy, and self-possession, qualities, indeed which are almost implied in the success of a nurse or medical woman. She might have practiced medicine with success and her care of the patients did, in fact, involve the practice of medicine.

The Brown Families

No person since the death of her first patron, Dr. Sanborn, has caused by death so great a loss to the town and to her own circle of friends in all parts of the country. Her unfailing cheerfulness and humor, and her profound knowledge of human nature, united with high ability and complete unselfishness, distinguished her whereever she was known, but her way of life kept her from being so familiarly known in her own town as might otherwise have been the case. She had along with other gifts the talent of owning land and leaves a considerable estate to her heirs.

On 23 March 1915 William H. Brown and Margaret Smith adopted a minor child, William Henry White, changing his surname to Brown (P).

Ten years later William H. Brown, the father, made the following will:

I, William Brown of Hampton Falls, in the County of Rockingham, and State of New Hampshire, make, publish and declare this as and for my last will and testament, hereby revoking all wills heretofore made by me.

After the payment of my just debts and funeral charges, I give, devise and bequeath as follows:

To my wife, Margaret Smith Brown all of the property of which I shall die seized and possessed including any property over which I may have power of appointment.

I nominate my wife, Margaret Smith Brown to be executrix of this my will and I request that she be exempted from giving surety or sureties on her bond as such executrix. I give said executrix full power and authority to sell both real and personal estate by public auction or private sale.

In testimony whereof I hereunto set my hand and seal in the presence of three witnesses, declare and publish this to be my last will this 25th day of April, 1925.

Signed: William H. Brown

Witnesses: Mrs. Julia A. Swett, Mrs. Mabel I. Swett, and Edward L. Swett all of Dedham, Mass.

The *Exeter News-Letter* of 28 May 1926 carried the following obituary for William H. Brown:

BROWN - William Brown, a member of the Church and I.O.O.F., passed away, Monday, May 17 at 4 P.M., after a lingering case of artero sclerosis. Patiently he has been cared for by his devoted loved ones and their friends. His faith has never wavered. In his casket he looked as if he were on the lounge after returning from Church.

100

The Brown Families

Many relatives survive him. His neighbors speak of
him as a most accommodating man, willing in his strength
to leave and assist anyone who might need him.
    His funeral was largely attended and loving friends
bore him to the grave Wednesday at 2 P.M.

Margaret (Smith) Brown survived her husband. In 1933 she
was residing in Buzzard's Bay in Massachusetts (P). She died
in Chestnut Hill, Mass. in 1959. She and her husband are buried
in Brookside Cemetery in Hampton Falls where the inscriptions
read:

William H. Brown 1856-1926
Margaret S. Brown 1870-1959

The gravestone of Ellen (Dow) Brown is in the lot of her
parents in the Hampton Falls Churchyard Cemetery:

Ellen Dow, wife of William H. Brown
27 March 1849 - 24 July 1905

BROWN child (adopted):

WILLIAM HENRY - born Boston, Mass. on 28 Feb 1910, the
    son of Mary White (P). He was adopted by William H.
    and Margaret (Smith) Brown on 23 May 1915 (P). In
    1933 he resided at 47 Dwight Street in Boston, Mass.
    (P). He was a chauffeur.

#+#+#+#+#+#+#+#+#+#+#+#+#+#+#

WILLIAM SMITH BROWN was born at Manchester, N.H. on
12 August 1940, the son of Clyde W. and Ruth (Brown) Brown.
He graduated from Central High School in Manchester, N.H. and
served two years in the U.S. Army at Ft. Lewis in Washington
State. He has worked as a lineman for the Seward Construction
Company of Kittery, Me. On 6 September 1969 he married Joan
Teresa Nerbonne in Manchester, N.H. She was born there on 18
October 1946, the daughter of Henry and Sophie (Kowalczyk)
Nerbonne. She graduated from Memorial High School in Man-
chester and then entered Notre Dame College where she received
a B.A. degree in Biology. Subsequently she received Certifica-
tion and Registration in Medical Technology at Notre Dame
Hospital in Manchester from the American Society of Clinical
Pathologists, and worked at the Sacred Heart Hospital as a
Medical Technologist. They resided in Auburn, N.H. about 1981.
No children.

A SCOTTISH GAZETTEER

The following material describing the localities in Scotland mentioned in the text of the genealogies was transcribed from *Topographical Dictionary of Scotland* by Samuel Lewis, (London:1846), 2 Vols. Since the date of this work corresponds approximately with the date at which William Brown removed from Ireland to Scotland with his family, it provides an especially appropriate description of the area in which they and the other related families depicted in this genealgy lived and worked. The available data is listed below in alphabetical arrangement:

GLASSERTON - a parish, in the county of Wigton, 1 3/4 mile S.W. from Whithorn; containing, with the village of Monrieth, 1253 inhabitants. The name of the place is thought to signify, in the Saxon language, "a bare hill;" and it is supposed that the term was adopted from the number of bare hills in the vicinity. Very little is known of the early history of the parish. It is said, however, that St. Ninian, here usually called St. Ringan, the founder of Whithorn Priory, and the first bishop of Galloway, resided for a time in a cave on the shore at Physgill, for the purpose of mortification or penance; and the cave, which is arched with stones, is still vulgarly called St. Ringan's cave. The present parish was formed by the union of the lands of Glasserton and Kirkmaiden. The walls of Kirkmaiden church are yet in existance, on the shore, near Monrieth; and it is clear that it was formerly a distinct parish; though when it was united with Glasserton cannot be ascertained. The parish is about eight miles in length, varying in breadth from one to three miles, and contains 13,477 acres. It has the parish of Mochrum on the west; Sorbie and Kirkinner on the north; Whithorn on the east; and the bay of Luce on the south. Its coast, which is bold and rugged, and broken by numerous headlands and green peaks, lies

103

parallel with the north coast of the Isle of Man, the island being between sixteen and eighteen miles south of Glasserton. The general appearance of the county is unequal, the ground presenting a succession of heights and hollows. There is a small lake near Castle-Stewart house, in the north, in which are found eels, trout, pike, and perch; the loch of Dowalton, also, forms a small part of the boundary of the parish; and the road from Stranraer to Newton-Stewart intersects it.

The soil varies very considerably in different parts. On the lands in the north it is damp and poor, having a tenacious subsoil of till, which holds the moisture too near the surface; in the more southern parts it is a gravelly loam, frequently mixed with clay and moss. Between 7000 and 8000 acres are under cultivation; the waste extends over about 3000, and from 200 to 300 are planted. The crops follow the rotation of oats; potatoes or turnips; ryegrass and clover, with wheat and barley; and a crop of hay; after which the ground returns to pasture. Agriculture has been much improved within the last thirty years, especially since the practice of raining green crops became general. Much moss and heath have been brought into cultivation; and the natural obstacles to good farming arising from the nature of the soil have been successfully treated by skill and perseverance. The proper application of manure, and the attentions paid to division and inclosures, have also contributed to produce a highly advanced state of husbandry, and have amply rewarded the labour of the cultivator. Dairy-farming is pursued in many parts in preference to breeding, on account of its greater profit; the cows are chiefly the Ayrshire. The sheep in most repute are the Leicesters and the Highland breed; a few, purchased at Falkirk, are fattened on turnips during the winter. The cattle are the black Galloways, for which the parish has always been famous. The rateable annual value of Glasserton is Ł8519. The subsoil of the lands is for the most part strong till and rock, clay, and gravel, presenting many impediments to agricultural improvements, which can only be successfully met by a highly efficient system of husbandry: the strata are the greywacke rock, among which a piece of granite is occasionally found. In the parish are the mansions of Glasserton and Physgill, both handsome modern erections.

The ecclesiastical affairs are governed by the presbytery of Wigton and synod of Galloway, and the patronage is in the Crown; the stipend of the minister is Ł202, with a good manse, built in 1818, and a glebe of fifteen acres, valued at Ł20 per annum. The church is remarkable for the beauty of its situation, in Glasserton park, a tract of 150 acres thickly spread with ornamental plantations, among which, in different directions, a variety of single trees majestically rise, giving a bold relief to the picturesque scenery. The edifice, erected in the early part of the eighteenth century, was repaired, and enlarged by the addition of an aisle and a handsome tower, in 1836, and now contains 400 sittings. There is a parochial school, the master of which has a salary of Ŀ34, and about Ŀ20 fees, with a good house, built in 1825. Another school is supported, the master of which has a salary of Ŀ15, and fees; the salary arises from the gratuities of two ladies, and the school and master's house stand on land granted by the Earl of Stair rent-free. The poor have the interest of two sums, one of Ŀ1000, and the other of Ŀ60. Not long since was discovered, in a marl-pit on the estate of Castlewig, in Whithorn parish, but near the border of Glasserton, the head of a urus, which was sent to Sir Walter Scott, and is yet to be seen at Abbotsford.

GLENLUCE – a parish, in the county of Wigton, containing 2448 inhabitants, of whom 890 are in the village, ten miles S.E. from Stranraer. This parish anciently included New Luce, the two places together forming the parish of Leuce or Glenluce, which was divided in 1646 into two parts, one called New, and the other Old. The abbey of Glenluce, situated in the deep valley of the river Luce, founded in 1190 by Roland Macdonald, Lord of Galloway, the Constable of Scotland, and covering a large space of ground, was the abode of Cistercian monks who came from Melrose. It was converted, however, in 1602, by James VI, into a temporal barony, in favor of Lawrence Gordon, abbot of the place; and on the death of Lawrence, it was bestowed by royal charter on his elder brother, John, Dean of Salisbury, who, dying in 1619, was succeeded in the barony by his son-in-law Sir Robert Gordon, the historian. Subsequently it was annexed to the see of Galloway; and at the close of the 17th century, being again made a barony, it conferred the title of Lord Glenluce, upon Sir James Dalrymple of Carrick, whose son became Lord Glenluce and Earl of Stair. Thomas Hay had been, in 1560, appointed commendator of the abbey, by a bull from the Pope; and from him Sir James Dalrymple Hay, of Park, the present proprietor of the abbey, is descended.

The parish is ten miles long and eight miles broad, and contains 40,350 acres. It is bounded on the north by New Luce; on the south by the Bay of Luce; on the east by Mochrum and Kirkowan; and on the west by Inch and Stonykirk. Except in the immediate neighborhood of the bay, the surface of the land is irregular and hilly. Besides a considerable number of perennial springs, the water of which, coming from rocks, is unusually clean and cold, there are several small lakes, and the two rivers Luce and Pooltanton, the former of which is here about thirty feet wide. It runs for twenty-one miles from its source in Ayrshire, and empties itself into the bay almost at the same place as the stream of Pooltanton. In each of these rivers salmon and sea-trout are taken. The soil varies to a considerable extent, but that which prevails most is of a gravelly or sandy nature, and is light and dry; the best land is found in the southern parts, and in the vicinity of the river Luce. In some places the soil contains large mixtures of moss, clay, or loam, and runs to a depth of two or three feet. The annual crops are as follows: 400 acres of wheat, 1350 of oats, 454 rye-grass, 259 meadow-hay, 60 peas and beans, 467 potatoes, and 160 turnips. About 10,000 acres are uncultivated, and betwen 300 and 400 are wood. Within the last thirty years the agricultural appearance of the parish has undergone a total change. Large quantities of waste land have been brought into cultivation, and the increase of dairies, supplying plenty of manure, together with the prevalence of the green-cropping system, has produced the most beneficial effect. In most parts suited for pasture, especially among the moors, cattle of the black Galloway breed are preferred, and the sheep most esteemed are of the black-faced breed, with horns, and producing long course wool. In the south are some superior dairy-farms, where more than 6000 stone of cheese are made every year. The farm buildings are in general commodious, and in good condition. The subsoil of the parish is gravelly or sandy, except in the heavier soils, and sinks to a very considerable depth: the rocks are ordinary greywacke, intermixed with quartz, and granite is found in almost every direction. A greywacke quary in the vicinity of the village has been wrought for some years, to the great advantage of the parish. The rateable annual value of Old Luce is Ŀ10,232.

There are three Castles, viz., the Castle of Park, the former residence of the Hays, Castle Synniness; and Carsecreuch, once the residence of the earls of Stair: but of these seats only one is entire. Genoch and Balkail are modern mansions. The village is situated upon the road leading from Newton-Stewart to Stranraer. Corn and carding-mills are regularly at work; there are also a dye-mill and a flax-mill. Cattle-markets are held near the village, from April to December, on the first Friday in each month, and a fair in the month of May; there is a regular post in the village, and the mail from Dumfries to Portpatrick runs through it every day. Within two miles of it is a harbour in the bay, suited to receive small craft bringing coal and lime; but no larger vessels can approach this part of the shore. The ecclesiastical affairs are subject to the presbytery of Stranraer and synod of Galloway, and the patronage is in the Crown; the stipend of the minister is Ŀ158, of which nearly half is received from the exchequer, with a manse, and a glebe valued at Ŀ30 per annum. The church, erected in 1814, is a commodious edifice, and situated close to the village. The members of the United Secession have a place of worship. The master of the parochial school has a salary of Ŀ25.13, with a house and garden; and his fees average between L30 and L40. There are several other schools, of which two are connected with dissenters, and one is supported by the Hay family. The chief remains of antiquity are the abbey ruins; the chapter-house is still in good condition, and its arches are distinguished by antique figures of white free-stone. The celebrated characters connected with the parish have been, John Gordon, Dean of Salisbury, eminent for numerous literary works; Sir Robert Gordon, the historian; and the Rev. Robert McWard, a theological and controversial writer in the reigns of Charles I and II, and who was at one time secretary to the well-known Samuel Rutherford.

KIRKINNER - a parish in the county of Wigton containing, with the hamlets of Marchfarm and Slohabert, 1769 inhabitants, of whom 229 are in the village of Kirkinner, three miles S.W. of Wigton. This place, which is of very remote antiquity, derives its name from the virgin saint Kinneir, by whom its ancient church was consecrated, and who suffered martyrdom at Cologne in 450. The church was granted by Edward Bruce, Lord of Galloway, to the priory of Whithorn; and on its resignation by the brethren of that establishment to James V in 1503, in exchange for the church of Kirkandrews, it was attached to the chapel royal of Stirling. Subsequently, it formed the benefice of the sub-dean of the chapel. The original parish included the whole of the district now forming the parish of Kirkowan, after the separation of which, the ancient parish of Longcastle was united with Kirkinner on the decay of its church, which fell into ruin in 1630. The early history of the place is not distinquished by any other events of importance. The old castle of Baldoon, for nearly two centuries the seat of the Dunbar family, and which furnished Sir Walter Scott with incidents for his tale of the "Bride of Lammermoor", passed, by marriage to the heiress, to the Hamiltons, and then to the Douglases, with whom it remained till 1793, when the estate was purchased by the Earl of Galloway.

The parish is bounded on the east by the bay of Wigton, along which it extends for about three miles, and on the north by the river Bladenoch; and comprises 15,000 acres, of which 13,500 are arable, 300 woodland and plantations, and the remainder hill pasture, moor, and moss. The surface along the shore of the bay is perfectly level, but in most other parts is diversified with gentle undulations, and hills of moderate height, sometimes covered with verdue, or crowned with plantations, which add much to the beauty of the scenery. The bay is here from seven to eight miles in width at high water, but retires, at the ebb of the tide, to a considerable distance from the shore, leaving a level tract of sand more than a mile in breadth. The river Bladenock has its source near the borders of Ayrshire, and flows in a winding course into Wigton bay; it abounds with salmon, trout, and sperlings, and is navigable for nearly two miles from its mouth. The other streams in the parish are the Malzie and the Mildriggen; the former joins the Bladenoch soon after that river enters the parish, on the west, and the latter flows north-eastward through the grounds of Bladenoch and Baldoon park, into the Bladenoch near its influx into the bay. At the south-western extremity of the parish is the lake of Dowalton, or Longcastle,, a sheet of water about two miles in length and a mile and a half in breadth, of which the larger portion is in the parish of Sorby. Pike and perch are found in the lake; and on the Kirkinner side at a small distance from the shore, are two small islands, one of which is thirty acres in extent. There are numerous springs of excellent water in various parts of the parish, and also some of which the water is strongly impregnated with iron; the principal of these is on the lands of Barnbarroch, and was formerly much resorted to by invalids.

The most prevailing soil is of gravelly nature; on the low lands of Baldoon are some large alluvial tracts. In others are patches of moss; but the lands generally have been greatly enriched by the use of shellmarl for manure, of which abundant supplies are obtained from the shores of the bay. The crops are, oats, wheat, barley, potatoes, and turnips, with the various grasses; the system of husbandry is in an improved state, and a due rotation of crops is carefully observed. The lands have been drained, and inclosed partly with fences of thorn and partly with dykes of stone; the farm-houses and offices are substantial and well-arranged, and many of them of superior order. The cattle reared are usually of the Galloway breed, and great attention is paid to their improvement; large numbers are annually fattened for the Liverpool market, and shipped at Wigton. Few sheep are bred; but many of the Highland kind, purchased at the Falkirk tryst, are fed on turnips during the winter and spring, and afterwards sent to Whitehaven and Liverpool, where they find a ready sale. The plantations, which are mostly of modern growth, consist of firs, interspersed with various sorts of forest trees, for which the soil is well adapted; they are under careful management, and in a thriving state, especially the beech, ash, plane, and Huntingdon willow, of which many have attained a luxuriant growth. The prevailing rocks are of the transition kind, and boulders of granite are found in some places; but stone of good quality for building is very scarce, and there are not any mines or quarries. The rateable annual value of Kirkinner is Ł10,997. Barnbarroch House, the seat of the Agnew family is a stately modern mansion, situated nearly in the center of the parish, in an extensive and richly-planted demesne. The village is on the road that leads to Wigton; a few of the inhabitants are employed in weaving linen by hand-looms at their own dwellings. A post-office has been established here, and has a daily delivery; and facility of communication is maintained by good roads, which intersect the parish, and by bridge over the various streams, of which that across the river Bladenoch is a substancial structure. At Baldoon is a small harbour, for the accomodation of vessels bringing supplies of coal and other articles required in the district, and for the shipment of grain, cattle and other agricultural produce.

The ecclesiastical affairs are under the superintendence of the presbytery of Wigton and synod of Galloway. The minister's stipend is £230, with a manse, and a glebe valued at £20 per annum, patrons, the Agnew family. The church, erected in 1828, is a handsome and substancial structure containing 800 sittings, and is situated at a small distance to the east of the village.

The parochial school is well conducted, and attended by about 100 children; the master has a salary of £34, with a house and garden, and the fees average £30 per annum. The schoolhouse is a spacious building near the church, and contains a small library for the use of the scholars. At Cairnfield was a Druidical circle of which the stones have long been removed; and in a cairn near the site, which has also been taken down and the stones used for building fences, were found, inclosed in a coffin of rudely-formed slabs, human bones partly consumed by fire. There are vestiges of two circular camps, of which the history is unknown; and not far from Loch Dowalton are some remains of the ancient church of Longcastle. Numerous ancient coins have been found at different times on the farm of Barness. Of the family of Vaux, formerly proprietors of Barnbarroch, Alexander was consecrated Bishop of Galloway in 1426, and in 1429 was appointed by James I one of the conservators of peace on the Scottish borders; his cousin, George Vaux, was bishop of Galloway in the reign of James III. Sir Patrick Vaux, the last distinquished member of the family, was made Lord of sesseon by James VI, and was subsequently sent by that monarch as ambassador to the court of Denmark.

MOCHRUM - a parish, in the county of Wigton, containing, with the villages of Eldrig, Kirk of Mochrum, and Port-William, 2539 inhabitants, of whom 187 are in the village of Kirk of Mochrum, 7 1/2 miles S.W. from Wigton. This place, of which the name is altogether of unknown derivation, appears to have formed part of the possessions of the Dunbar family, having been conferred about the year 1368 upon the second son of Patrick, Earl of Mar, their ancestor. Among his descendants, who were subsequently raised to the dignity of baronets, the most distinquished was Gavin, son of Sir John Dunbar, who, having devoted himself to study, was in 1504 made prior of Whithorn, and in 1522 succeded James Beaton as archbishop of Glasgow. In 1526 he was made lord chancellor of Scotland, and in 1536 was chosen one of the lords of the regency during the absence of James V at the court of France while celebrating his marriage with Magdalene, daughter of Francis I. The original residence of the Dunbars, knights of Mochrum, an ancient castle called the Old Place of Mochrum, of which the walls, of great strength, are still nearly entire, is situated in the vicinity of an extensive moor surrounded with numerous lakes, and has an interesting and picturesque appearance. The castle, and the lands attached to it, remained in the possession of the Dunbars till towards the close of the last century, when they passed to the earls of Dumfries; and subsequently to the present Marquess of Bute; but the title of baronets of Mochrum is still retained by their descendants, whose representative is Sir William Rowe Dunbar, Bart. With the exception of the lands appertaining to the Old Place, nearly one-half of the parish is the property of the Maxwells, who settled here in the early part of the 17th century, and whose representative is Sir William Maxwell, Bart.

The parish is bounded on the south-west by the bay of Luce, and is nearly ten miles in length and from four to five miles in breadth, comprising 22,000 acres, of which 200 are woodland and plantation, about 1000 waste, and the remainder, almost in equal proportions, meadow, pasture, and arable land in good cultivation. The surface, though not rising into hills of any considerable elevation, is boldly undulating, and diversified with tracts of level land and gentle acclivities in pleasing variety; and the higher grounds command a fine view, extending over the bay of Luce and the Irish Channel, and embracing the Mull of Galloway, the Isle of Man, the mountains of Morne on the Irish coast, and the heights of Skiddaw in Cumberland. Towards the north-west are numerous lakes, of which the most important are Mochrum and Castle lochs, each about a mile and a quarter in length and a quarter of a mile in width, and containing islets of picturesque appearance. From there, and also from the smaller lakes, issue many riverlets intersecting the lands in various directions; and some uniting their streams, form the Malzie water, which flows eastward through the parish into the Bladenoch, and is the only water approaching in character to a river. The coast extends nearly ten miles, and for the greater part is a flat smooth gravelly beach about fifty yards in width, but is bounded by a precipetous bank rendering communication with the interior difficult, and at about a mile from the western extremity terminates in a steep rock projecting into the bay, and forming a bold and almost inaccessible shore. There are several indentations or creeks affording shelter to boats; but the only harbour accessible to trading vessels of any considerable burthen is Port-William, near the eastern extremity of the bay, which has safe anchorage for vessels of 200 tons, and was constructed during the last century by Sir William Maxwell. The bay abounds with fish of almost every variety, and of excellent quality; salmon and herrings are taken in moderate quantities, and cod, mackerel, whiting, and other white-fish are found in considerable numbers.

The soil along the coast is mostly a rich deep loam, alternated with patches of lighter quality; towards the central part it gradually becomes thin and stony; and in the west and east are some tracts of moor and moss, with intervening portions of dry and fertile arable land. The system of husbandry has been greatly improved under the auspices of Sir William Maxwell, liberal encouragement being afforded to his tennants; favorable crops of all kinds of grain are raised, and considerable numbers of cattle and sheep are reared. The farms are well inclosed, chiefly with hedges of thorn; the farm houses and offices are generally substantial and commodiously arranged, and all the more recent improvements in the construction of agricultural implements have been adopted. The plantations, though not extensive, add much to the scenery, and such of them as are sheltered from the sea breezes are in a thriving state; but the soil does not appear to be adapted to their extension. The rateable annual value of the parish is Ł8980. Monrieth House, the seat of Sir William Maxwell, is a modern mansion, situated on an eminence near the eastern boundary of the parish about a mile from the sea, and at the head of a small but beautiful lake surrounded with plantations. Myrton Cottage, a handsome residence was built by the same gentleman within the last few years. The village of Mochrum, in which the church stands, is neatly built; and its inhabitants are chiefly employed in agricultural pursuits. The village of Eldrig and Port-William are described under their respective heads; at Port-William is a post-office which has six deliveries in the week, and facility of intercourse is maintained by good roads, of which the turnpike-road to Glenluce passes along the coast for several miles, opening a communication with the Rhinns of Galloway. The ecclesiatical affairs are under the superintendence of the presbytery of Wigton and synod of Galloway. The minister's stipend is Ł153-3-5, with a manse, and a glebe valued at Ł25 per annum; patron, the Crown. The church, built in 1794, and successively enlarged by the addition of gallaries in 1822 and 1832, is a substantial structure containing 700 sittings. There is a place of worship for members of the Relief. The parochial school is well attended; the master receives the minimum salary, with the allowance in lieu of a house, and the fees average about Ł16 annually. The schoolroom is a handsome building, adopted for the reception of 150 children. Near the church is a large earthen mound surrounded by a deep fosse. On the summit of an eminence not far from the eastern extremity of the coast, are some very distinct traces of an Anglo-Saxon camp; and near the shore, about two miles from the western extremity, are the ruins of the ancient chapel of St. Finian.

A Scottish Gazetteer

MONRIETH - A village, in the parish of Glasserton, county of Wigton, 6 miles W. from Whithorn; containing 94 inhabitants. This is a small village situated near a creek or bay of the same name, on the west coast of the parish, and opening into the bay of Luce. The road from Whithorn passes through the village to Port-William, about two miles north-westward of it. At a short distance, near the sea-shore, are some remains of the ancient church of Kirkmaiden; they consist of the walls, which are still pretty entire.

PORT-WILLIAM - a village, in the parish of Mochrum, county of Wigton, 8 1/2 miles S.W. from Wigton; containing 634 inhabitants. This is a neat and thriving sea-port village, situated on the eastern shore of Luce Bay; it was built about 1762 by Sir William Maxwell, Bart., of Monrieth, in honour of whom it is named. In 1788 small barracks were erected here for military, and for custom-house affairs, in order to facilitate the prevention of contraband trade. The harbour is safe and commodious, and from it large quantities of potatoes and grain are shipped for Liverpool and Lancaster. The bay abounds with fish of excellent quality, and in great variety. In the village is a post-office, which has a daily delivery.

SORBIE - a parish, in the district of Machers, county of Wigton, 6 miles S. from Wigton; containing with the village of Garliestown and Sorbie, 1700 inhabitants, of whom 809 are in the rural districts, and 235 in the village of Sorbie. This place comprehends the three ancient parishes of Sorbie, Kirkmadrine, and Cruggleton, which were united about the middle of the 17th century. It is supposed to have derived its name, originally "Sourby", signifying in the Saxon language "a gloomy habitation", from the situation of the castle on the confines of a cold and dreary marsh that has been since drained and brought under cultivation. The castle of Sorbie, of which there are now but very inconsiderable remains, belonged, together with the lands attached to it, to the family of the Hannays in the reign of James IV, and continued in their possession till about the commencement of the present century; the Earl of Galloway is now the principal landed proprietor. The castle of Cruggleton, from which that parish took its name, and of which only some of the foundations of the walls, and part of an arch, are at present left, was seated on the summit of a bold promontory near the mouth of Wigton bay; and is said to have been the baronial residence of John Cumyn, Earl of Buchan, in the 13th century, as one of the coheirs of the ancient lords of Galloway. In 1292, the Earl obtained from Edward I of England licence to procure lead in the Calf of Man, for the roofing of his castle of Crugglton, which, after his subsequent defeat by Robert Bruce, was, with

112

the neighboring lands, forfeited to the crown. Of its subsequent history little is known; it became a ruin towards the close of the 17th century, and the estate is now the property of Sir Andrew Agnew, of Lochnaw, Bart.

The parish is bounded on the east by Wigton bay, and is about six miles in extreme length, varying from three miles and a half to nearly six miles in breadth, and comprising 9000 acres, of which 7700 are arable with a moderate proportion of meadow and pasture, 400 woodland and plantations, and the remainder moor and waste. The surface is diversified with hills of moderate elevation, interspersed with fertile valleys, and commanding from their summits fine views of the bay of Wigton, Solway Firth, the Cumberland mountains, and the Isle of Man. The prevailing scenery, enlivened with flourishing plantations, is agreeably varied,and in some parts picturesque. There are no rivers of any importance; but on the north-western boundary is Loch Dowlton, so called from the former proprietor of the lands, a fine sheet of water more than three miles in circumference and varying from six to twenty feet in depth. From this lake, which abounds with pike, perch, and eels, issues a small stream which intersects the parish from west to east, and flows into Garliestown bay; and in various parts of the parish are perennial springs, affording an ample supply of excellent water. The coast, including its several windings, is about twelve miles in extent; and is indented with numerous bays, of which the principal are those of Garliestown and Rigg, whereof the latter, in compliment to Capt. Hunter, of the royal navy, who brought his ship to anchor there, has since been sometimes called Hunter's bay; on the north is Orchardton bay, which is dry at low water. The bay of Garliestown is well adapted for the construction of a spacious harbour, which would greatly facilitate the trade between the western coast of England and this country. The smaller bays are, Innerwell, Allan, and Whapple; and the principal headlands, Eagerness, Innerwell, and Cruggleton Points, of which Eagerness Point is the most prominent. The shore on the north, and at Garlietown and Rigg, is flat and sandy; at Eagerness it is rocky, but not precipitous; while from the south-east of Rigg bay to Whithorn it is bold and precipitous, rising in some places abruptly to a height of 200 feet above the level of the sea. The rocks on this part of the coast are perforated with two nearly contiguous caves, each about 120 feet in depth, and both having arched roofs of great beauty, naturally formed in the solid rock; the one is 100 feet in height and thrity-six in width, and the other forty feet high and fifteen feet wide. A salmon-fishery is carried on at Port-Innenwell, which produces an annual rental of Ł200 to the proprietors; and herrings, mackerel, cod, and various other kinds of fish are also taken here in abundance. Herrings were likewise found some few years since off Garlietown, and many of the inhabitants engaged in the fishery; but, from recent want of success, it has been almost discontinued.

The soil is generally light, but fertile, and in a high state of cultivation; the crops are, oats, barley, a little wheat, some potatoes, and turnips, with the usual grasses. The system of husbandry has been much improved of late, and bone-dust has been introduced with success. The farm houses and offices are mostly substancial and conveniently arranged, the lands inclosed, and the fences kept in good repair; the greatest encouragement is given to the tenantry by the proprietors, and the liberal terms on which the leases are granted afford a powerful stimulus to improvement. Great attention is paid to the management of live-stock. The sheep are of the common native breed, with a mixture of others; many of them are bought in at the Falkirk trysts, and, when fattened on turnips, sent to the Liverpool markets by steam-boats, for which the parish has every facility. The cattle are all of the Galloway breed; they are mostly of a black colour, without horns, and are usually sold when two or three years old to dealers who send them to Dumfries, where they are purchased for the supply of the English markets. The plantations comprise oak, ash, beech, birch, alder, plane, larch, and various kinds of firs, for all of which the soil appears to be well adapted; they are regularly thinned, and in a thriving state. In the grounds of Galloway House are some remarkably fine specimens of laurel, evergreen, turkey-oak, and horse-chesnut. The rocks are generally of the transition series; and the substrata, whinstone and gravel, with a few boulders of granite, which lie on the surface, and seldom exceed three feet in length. Neither ores nor minerals of any kind have been discovered, nor are there any quarries in operation. The rateable annual value of the parish is L8646. Galloway House, the seat of the Earl of Galloway, is a stately mansion erected about the middle of the 18th century, and beautifully situated on the coast, between the bays of Garlietown and Rigg, over both of which it commands an interesting view, with the Cumberland mountains and the Isle of Man in the distance. The house contains many spacious and elegant apartments tastefully embellished, and a library of many thousand volumes in the various departments of literature; the grounds are richly embellished with ancient timber and thriving plantation.

The village of Garlietown is described under its own head. That of Sorbie was commenced towards the close of the last century, under the auspices of the Earl of Galloway; it is situated nearly in the center of the parish; the houses are neatly built, and the environs abound with much pleasing scenery. The manufacture of damask was established here about fifty years since, and was brought to very great perfection, both for fineness of texture, and beauty and variety of patterns; the damask was made from the best Dutch flax spun by hand, and the articles produced were in high repute throughout Scotland and England. Some damask manufactured here in 1800 was sent to Edinburgh, and submitted for competition at the annual meeting of the Board of Trustees, where it obtained the highest premium; and complete suits of table-linen have been prepared at this place for most of the noble families in the kingdom. The manufactory afforded employment to about 100 persons, including both weavers and spinners. There are still rope and sail works at Garlietown, and some shops in the village of Sorbie for the supply of the inhabitants. Letters are delivered daily from the post-office of Wigton; and facility of communication is maintained by good roads, which intersect the parish in various directions, and by steam-boats and other vessels, which frequent the harbour of Garlietown. The ecclesiastical affairs are under the superintendence of the presbytery of Wigton and synod of Galloway; the minister's stipend is Ł244.13.7, with a manse, and a glebe valued at Ł15 per annum; patron, the Crown. The church, situated in the village, was rebuilt in 1750, and repaired in 1826; it is a neat substancial structure containing 500 sittings. The members of the Free Church have a place of worship; and there is a place of worship at Garlietown for Independents. The parochial school is well conducted, and attended by about sixty children; the master has a salary of Ł33.3, with a house and garden, and the fees average Ł20 annually. There are several other schools, of which two, at Garlietown, are endowed by the Earl and Counters of Galloway. Some remains exist of the ancient church of Kirkmadrine, which appears to have been a very small structure; the old churchyard is still used as a burying-ground by some families. Patrick Hannay, a poet of some eminence, was a native of this parish: a volume of his poems, published in 1662, was recently sold in London for the sum of L -42.10.6.

WHITHORN - a royal burgh and a parish, in the county of Wigton, 11 miles S. from Wigton, and 97 1/2 S. by W. from Glasgow, containing, with the village of Isle of Whithorn, 2795 inhabitants, of whom 495 are in Isle of Whithorn, and 1502 in the burgh. This place, which occupies the south-eastern extremity of the county, is of remote antiquity, being identified as the "Leucophibia" of Ptolemy, during the Roman occupation of Britain, and as subsequently the capital of the "Novantes", who made themselves masters of the whole of Galloway. It seems to have derived its present name from the erection of a church here by St. Ninian in the 4th century, which, being the first in the country that was built of white freestone, obtained from its light appearance the appellation of "Candida Casa". In the eighteenth century the place became the seat of the ancient bishops of

Galloway; and it continued to be the head of that diocese after its revival in the 12th century. Fergus, Lord of Galloway, in the reign of David I founded here a priory for Praemonstratensian Canons, of which the church was appropriated as the cathedral of the see. This establishment was eminent from the possession of the relics of St. Ninian, and for centuries before the Reformation was the frequent resort of devotees on their pilgrimage to visit the shrine of that state, among whom were some of the Scottish sovereigns.

In 1425, James I granted full protection to all strangers coming into Scotland for that purpose; and in 1473, Margaret, queen of James III, attended by a retinue of ladies of her household, made a pilgrimage to the shrine. James IV during his reign paid frequent visits to the church, on which occasions he presented numerous offerings in honour of the saint; and his son and successor, James V, in the years 1532 and 1533 performed pilgrimages to the shrine, which, even for a considerable time after the Reformation, continued to attract devotees. Among the most distinguished of the priors of this establishment were Gavin Dunbar, afterward Arcbishop of Glasgow, and James Beaton, Archbishop of St. Andrew's, and Chancellor of Scotland. The priory flourished till the Dissolution in 1561, when its revenues amounted to Ł1016 in money, and various payments in kind. Of the ancient buildings there are but very inconsiderable remains, consisting chiefly of some arches of the church, one of which, however, almost entire, is a remarkably fine specimen of Saxon architecture.

The town, which is situated almost in the center of the parish, consists principally of one spacious street more than half a mile in length, which towards the center expands into unusually great breadth, and from which diverge two or three smaller streets and lanes. The houses are generally neatly built, and roofed with slate; many of the more ancient have been taken down, and rebuilt in a better style; and various other improvements have recently been made in the appearance of the place. The principal street is intersected nearly in the middle by a rivulet, over which is a neat bridge. There are no manufactures carried on; and the only trade is that which the town derives from its proximity to the small port of Isle of Whithorn, which is separately described, and from the usual handicrafts requisite for the supply of the neighborhood. Branches of the Bank of Scotland and the Edinburgh and Glasgow Bank, and an agency for the Aberdeen Insurance office, have been established, and a fair, chiefly for hiring servants, is held annually in Midsummer, and a cattle market monthly from April to January. The town was erected into a royal Burgh by charter of King Robert Bruce, which was confirmed by charter of James IV in 1571. The government is vested in a provost, two bailies, and fifteen councillors; but there are no incorporated trades possessing exclusive privileges, and every inhabitant is free to carry on trade within the burgh. The magistrates have the usual jurisdiction of burghs royal; but no civil causes are brought for their decision, and in crimminal matters their jurisdiction extends only to breaches of the peace. The town-hall, situated on the west side of the principal street, is a substantial structure with a tower and spire, and attached to it is a gaol, used as a place of temporary confinement. The burgh is associated with New Galloway, Stranraer, and Wigton, in returning a member to the imperial parliament; the number of qualified voters at present registered is fifty.

The parish is bounded on the south by the Irish Channel, and on the east by the bay of Wigton; it is about eight miles in extreme length, and varies from two to five miles in breadth, comprising an area of 10,000 acres, of which the whole, with the exception of about 200 acres of meadow and a little waste, is arable. The surface, though generally level, is marked by numerous hillocks of various form and appearance, most of them covered with briars and whim, which give to the parish an aspect of sterility. There are no rivers of any importance; but three small burns flow through the lands into the sea, each of which in its course gives motion to some corn-mills; and there are numerous springs of clear water, of which one, on the Isle of Whithorn, is slightly chalybeate. The several lakes have been drained, and some of them brought under tillage: of those which have not been cultivated, some form peat-mosses, and others produce great quantities of excellent marl. The coast, which is more than nine miles in extent, is in some parts bold and rocky, especially towards Burrow Head, on the south, where many of the rocks rise perpendicularly from the sea to a height of 200 feet. Some of the rocks are perforated with deep caverns; and on the east are several bays, whereof the principal are, Port-Allan, Port-Yarrock, and the Isle of Whithorn, at which last there is a commodious harbor.

The soil is generally fertile, and in some parts a rich vegetable mould resting upon a bottom or rock; it has been much improved by a liberal use of bone-dust and guano as manure. The chief crops are, wheat, oats, barley, potatoes, and turnips. The system of husbandry is making steady progress; a due rotation of crops is uniformly observed; the farm-buildings are substancial, and roofed with slate, and the lands mostly inclosed with stone dykes. The cattle, once wholly of the Galloway breed, and to the improvement of which the greatest attention is paid, have since the increase of dairy-farms been partly of the Ayrshire breed; and considerable numbers are now fed on turnips till fit for the market, and sent by sea to Liverpool. The plantations are gradually increasing in extent, and at Castlewigg are some noble specimens of oak, ash, beech, and firs. An attempt was at one time unsuccessfully made to work coal; and at Tonderghie, copper of rich quality was discovered by a mining company from Wales, but the works have long been discontinued. The rateable annual value of the parish, according to returns made under the Income tax, is Ŀ10,313. Castlewigg, the seat of Hugh Hathorn, Esq., is an ancient and venerable mansion, beautifully situated in a richly-planted demesne, near the western border of the parish; and Tonderghie, near the southern coast, the seat of Hugh D. Stewart, Esq., is a handsome modern mansion, commanding a fine view of the English coast and the Isle of Man. The only village is Isle of Whithorn, which is described under its own head.

The ecclesiastical affairs are under the superintendence of the presbytery of Wigton, and synod of Galloway. The minister's stipend is Ŀ246.15.9, with a manse, and a glebe valued at Ŀ20 per annum; patron, the Crown. The church, erected on part of the site of the priory in 1822, is a substancial and neat structure containing 800 sittings: in the churchyard are the only remains of the priory and cathedral, conveying but a faint idea of the ancient grandeur of the buildings. There are places of worship for members of the Free Church, the Secession Synod, and Refomed Presbyterians, and a Roman Catholic chapel. Of the two parochial schools, one is in the burgh and the other at Isle of Whithorn: the master of the burgh school has a salary of Ŀ39, with Ŀ6.6 in lieu of a dwelling-house, and the other master a salary of Ŀ19.10; the school fees averaging Ŀ50 per annum in the aggregate. About half a mile to the west of the town are the remains of a Roman camp, and numerous Roman coins have been found near the priory, and in various other parts of the parish. On the shore are the ruins of several castles and fortresses, which supposed to have been built for the protection of the coast from the frequent incursions of the Scandinavians, who made the Isle of Man their common rendezvous in their predatory attacks on this part of the country.

DESCENDANT CHART

This chart is intended to help recent descendants see how they are related genetically to William Brown and his wife Isabella Kennedy. It shows all the their descendants presently known to the compilers. Active solicitaion of data from family members ended many years ago, so many lines are incomplete – there have been many births and marriages in recent years which could, no doubt, be added if the information were available. However, a project of this nature is by its very nature never complete.

The arrangement of this chart is quite obvious: with the exception of William Brown himself, all the men listed on the first line of each surname block married a descendant of William Brown, but are not themselves a descendant of William Brown. All their children, grandchildren, etc. shown with succesive levels of indentations are blood descendants of William Brown and Isabella Kennedy, except for a few adopted children who are identified as such where known.

Each line is intended to give only the barest essential genealogical data, i.e., the name, year of birth, place of birth, and name of spouse(s) in order to show have the various people are related to William Brown. Surnames given in captial letters indicate another connection to the chart and should make it an easy process for the recent generations to trace their line of descent. People have generally been identified by the name they were born with which may changed due to marriages and adoptions. An attempt has been made to list all the marriages of descendants of William and Isabella Brown, but no attempt has been made to list all the marriages of their spouses, of the many divorces, because of lack of space in this chart.e

All the available data on the descendants born with the surname BROWN are given in the genealogical articles elsewhere in this book, but much information has also been collected on many of the other descendants shown on this chart. Any descendant wishing to acquire photocopies of the files pertinent to his or her line of descent is welcome to write to the compilers at 3602 Maureen Lane, Bowie, MD 20715.

The information presented here has been collected from public records, newspaper announcements, and family sources, and may not always be totally accurate. The compilers apologize in advance for any errors of omission or commission.

ARGABRIGHT, Charles C - b Wheeling WV m Vivian DeLong BROWN
    Sharon Emerald - m W Dale Plummer
    Charlene DeLong - m Thomas Crowder
    Glenn Clyden -

AHEARN, Edward J - bc1910 Manchester NH m Gladys Bartlett BLOCK
    Robert Edward - b1931 dy

AJEMIAN, George - b1924 Lawrence MA m Gloria Ruth WHENAL
    Shari Lynne - b1949 Exeter NH
    Bonnie Susan - b1951 Exeter NH m Paul ROESSLER
    Dennis Alden - b1953 Exeter NH m Mary Ellen Binette
        Jennifer Rae - b1974 Exeter NH
        Rebecca Lynne - b1976 Exeter NH
        Matthew Dennis - b1978 Exeter NH
        Melissa Kate - b1980 Exeter NH
    Roxanne Esther - b1964 Exeter NH

AYERS, Clement Newton - b1882 Oakham MA m Marian G DEARBORN
    Marion Virginia - m1 Joseph LAFFEY m2 Harold Douglas Kilpatrick

BARKER, Earl Leslie - m Margaret Isabella DRYSDALE
    Nancy Jean - b1944 Exeter NH m Gary Wayne Sims
    Laura Margaret - b1946 Exeter NH m Fred McLeod
    Leslie William - b1947 Exeter NH

BARTLETT, Frank Herbert - b1859 Kingston NH m Isabelle Kimball BROWN
    Etta Pearl - b1889 Brentwood NH m John Albert BLOCK

BARTON, Robert - b Fall River MA m Jennie May WHEELOCK
   Isabel Brown - b1911 Fall River MA m Howard ROSE
   Glady Richmond - b1913 Fall River MA m1 Clifford LEACH m2 Dana Woodsome

BASTINE, Arthur G - m Doris Brown PORTER
   Robert J - b1940 Newburyport MA
   Jean M - b1942 Amesbury MA m Roland Stephan
   Ronald D - b1946 Amesbury MA
   James A - b1948 Amesbury MA

BERRY, Elmer Austin - b1888 Greenland NH m Clara E JENNESS
   Elmer R - b1910 Portsmouth NH m _____ Young
   Marjorie L - b1912 Portsmouth NH m Kelsey R Haynes no issue
   Verna E - b1914 Portsmouth NH m Glenn W SAWYER

BLATCHFORD, Earl - b1922 Exeter NH m Betty Jane BROWN
   Janet Elaine - b1949 Exeter NH m Joseph TROTTA
   Joyce Ann - b1951 Exeter NH

BLICKER, Carl Vincent - m Dorothy Jean BRISTOL
   Laura Leigh - b1964 Milton FL
   Brian Robert - b1966 Quonset RI

BLOCK, John Albert - b1883 Exeter NH m Etta Pearl BARTLETT
   Gladys Bartlett - b1910 Brentwood NH m Edward J AHEARN
   Evelyn Caroline - b1919 Brentwood NH m Warren Eastman Smith no issue
   Reginald Gordon - b1924 Exeter NH d WWII unm

BRAYALL, Arnold - m Anne Elizabeth WHENAL
   Richard Arnold - b1951 Portsmouth NH

BRALEY, Albert L - b Fairhaven MA m Jennie May WHEELOCK
   Albert L - b1920 Fairhaven MA m Aldine _____
      David Albert - b1965 New Bedford MA

BRISTOL, Myrle Elwood - b1911 Hampton NH m Gertrude Elizabeth BROWN
   Robert Alan - b1940 Portsmouth NH
   Dorothy Jean - b1941 Portsmouth NH m Carl Vincent BLICKER

BROWN, William - b1819 Ireland m Isabella Kennedy
   Benjamin B - b1837 Ireland m Elizabeth Thompson
      Alexander S - b1857 Scotland m Henrietta Maria Chapman
         Dora Elizabeth - b1882 Stratham NH m1 Clarence Harrison HOITT m2 Charles French
         William - b1859 Scotland
         Robert Livermore - b1861 Scotland m1 Ida Augusta Winn 1 ch m2 Isabella Wiseman
            Clarence Warren - b1883 Greenland NH m1 Thannie Wales Gleason 3 ch m2 Susie E Tebbetts
            Marion Beatrice - b1910 Marblehead MA m Norman S EWING
            Norman Robert - b1912 North Conway NH m Kathleen LaCoy
               G Geoffrey - b1941 Brooklyn NY m Karen Zeman
               Jill - b1946 Brooklyn NY m Bruce Fuller
               Norman Robert - b1950 Salem MA
               Judith A - b1959 Concord NH
            Richard Clarence - b1916 Portsmouth NH m Margaret Eleonore Mueller no issue
         John Durgin - b1862 Scotland m Elizabeth Elliott
            John William - b1891 Brentwood NH m1 Abbie E Anderson 3 ch m2 Elsie Bishop
            Alice Lena - b1912 Amesbury MA dy

Descendant Chart

BROWN (Continued)

Edith - b1914 Amesbury MA unm
John William - b1917 Amesbury MA m Eleanor _____
    Greg -
    John -
Ella Margaret - b1893 Brentwood NH m Thomas Bush WHITE
Lena Jane - b1895 Brentwood NH m Carlton L WELLS
Sarah Belle - b1897 dy
Anna Thompson - b1898 dy
Mabel Faith - b1899 Brentwood NH m Harold Carey PORTER
Isabell Wiseman - b1904 m1 Hartwell Berry REID m2 Chester Rohr
Benjamin Alexander - b1909 m1 Kathleen H Gorman m2 Evelyn Louise (Tate) Barrett no issue
Isabelle Kimball - b1864 Scotland m Frank Herbert BARTLETT
Andrew Garfield - b1866 Scotland m Nora Viva Holmes
    Clyde Lind - b1892 Nottingham NH m Charles Lester BUZZELL
    Nile Holmes - b1894 Rye Beach NH m1 Laura I Bousquet no issue m2 Emily Louise DeLong
        Marjorie Louise - b1919 Bridgeport CT m1 Willard BRUNT m2 Peter CARREIRO m3 Eugene Conti
        Bernice Arlene - b1921 m1 Kenneth I ESTABROOK m2 Robert A Meunier m3 Donald P Adams
        Vivian DeLong - b1925 New Haven CT m1 Charles C ARGABRIGHT m2 Johnnie S CLARK
        Nile Holmes - b1928 Bridgeport CT m Lorraine Meunier
            David Nile - b1950 Central Falls RI
            Arlene Barbara - b1955 Attleboro MA
            Jeffrey Robert - b1959 Fullerton CA
    Carl Garfield - b1929 dy
        Addison Orland - b1933 Bridgeport CT m Eva L (Beland) Batista
        Joyce Adele - b1936 Bridgeport CT m1 Leon R Isabelle m2 Louis DUARTE
Chester Jordan - b1901 Rye Beach NH dy
Benjamin B - b1867 Scotland m Annie Maynes

BROWN (Continued)

Howard George - b1890 Fremont NH m Jennie Mildred Watt
    Barbara Maynes - b1915 Haverhill MA m Leonard Joseph MARBLE
    Bremner Howard - b1922 Bradford MA m Marcia Merrow McCarthy
        Anne Jennifer - b1951 Lewiston ME d unm
        Marcia Frances - b1953 Haverhill MA
        Nancy Merrow - b1957 Haverhill MA
    son - b1892 d infant
    dau - b1893 d infant
    son - b1894 d infant
Elizabeth Campbell - b1869 Scotland m1 Charles OSGOOD m2 Ira PURINGTON m3 Wilbur A Shipley
Jennie Whenal - b1872 Brentwood NH m1 William H BURKE m2 Oscar MORRISON m3 Wm Sweetland
George Chester - b1875 Brentwood NH m May Lee
    Gertrude Elizabeth - b1902 Exeter NH m1 Harold L Johnston m2 Myrtle Elwood BRISTOL
    Morrill Howard - b1903 Exeter NH m Elva Lillian Hersey
        Shirley Ann - b1936 Wolfeborough NH m Leslie Hamilton COULTER
        Priscilla May - b1938 Wolfeborough NH m Robert Gienty no issue
        James Howard - b1945 Wolfeboro NH m Judith Ann Mulvey
    Lawrence George - b1907 Exeter NH unm
    Beatrice May - b1910 m1 Dwight Amos STANDISH m2 Mahlon Clough
Jane - b1839 Ireland m William WHENAL
Robert - b1843 Ireland m Janet Brown
    Robert - dy
    William - b1875 Hampton Falls NH m Cora Eva Blake
    Robert Orlando - b1898 Hampton NH m Helen Mae Kimball
    Betty Jane - b1924 Exeter NH m Earl BLATCHFORD
    Shirley - b1927 Portsmouth NH m Harlan Edward CARTER
    Clyde Wallace - b1899 Hampton NH m Ruth Amelia Brown

Descendant Chart

BROWN (Continued)

    Judith Lee - b1931 Newburyport MA m Arthur Russell PRENTISS

    Beverly June - b1933 Newburyport MA m Ralph J Bilodeau no issue

    William Smith - b1940 Manchester NH m Joan Nerbourne no issue

    Cora Hazel - b1901 Hampton NH m Norman Marston Coffin no issue

Mary Ann - b1846 Ireland m Joseph DRYSDALE

John - b1848 Scotland m Mary P Tarleton no issue but adopted

    Maude Aileen - b1888 Hampton Falls NH d/o Jonathan & Carrie (Emery) Perkins

Andrew - bc1851 Scotland dy

Martha - b1852 Scotland m Samuel Alonzo JENNESS

William Henry - b1856 Scotland m1 Ellen Dow m2 Margaret Smith no issue but adopted

    William Henry - b1910 Boston MA s/o Mary White

Andrew C - b1859 Scotland m Rose Matilda Glover no issue

Isabella - b1863 Scotland m William North WHEELOCK

BRUNT, Willard - m Marjorie Louise BROWN

    Carl Martin - b1937 Bridgeport CT m Jan _____

        son -

BURKE, William H - b1867 Canada m Jennie Whenal BROWN

    Jennie Mae - b1891 Brentwood NH m1 Walter H Dugay m2 George Edwin DEARBORN m3 F Stanley Walker

BURKLUND, Harold William - b1907 Manchester NH m Meryl Leola BUZZELL

    Marlene Adelaide - b1932 Raymond NH m Walter Vincent PAIGE

    Robert Lester - b1933 Northwood NH m Joan Ann Beauchain

        Debbie Lee - b1957 Rochester NH m Linwood Eric MARDEN

        Robin Leigh - b1958 Rochester NH m Richard E DROWN

        Robert Lester - b1962 Rochester NH

126

BURKLUND (Continued)
   Scott Gregg - b1963 Rochester NH m Meridith Winslow
   Carla Lind - b1946 Exeter NH m1 Clayton Woodbury DOWNING m2 Stephen A Blais

BUSSIERE, Leonard E - m Louise Rogers EVANS
   Mark Evans - b1951 Fitchburg MA
   Stephen - b1952 Fitchburg MA
   Scott - b1954 Fitchburg MA
   Gregory - b1955 Fitchburg MA
   George Russell - b1957 Fitchburg MA
   Amy Louise - b1961 Fitchburg MA

BUZZELL, Charles Lester - b1890 Newfields NH m Clyde Lind BROWN
   Meryl Leola - b1910 Exeter NH m Harold W BURKLUND
   Wilma Lois - b1913 Brookline MA m1 Gerald Charles TOWLE m2 John Joseph Regan
   Ruth - b1914 Brookline MA dy
   Ruth Irma - b1919 Worcester MA m1 Leo Francis McDONOUGH m2 Robert Henry SIMPSON

CARD, Robert Charles - b1921 Fall River MA m Helen Susan RICHARDSON
   Linda Sue - b1947 Fall River MA m Richard SILVIA
   Nancy Jean - b1949 Fall River MA
   Robert Charles - b1951 Fall River MA
   Paul Douglas - b1961 Fall River MA

CARREIRO, Peter - m Marjorie Louise BROWN
   Peter - b1949

CARTER, Harlan Edward - b1926 North Hampton NH m Shirley Ann BROWN

Descendant Chart

CARTER (Continued)
Paul Terry - b1946 Exeter NH m Mary Lou Robinson
    Matthew Paul - b1969
Sonjia Lee - b1947 Exeter NH m John J FARRINGTON
Harlan Edward - b1951 Exeter NH
Beverly Ann - b1954 Exeter NH
Robert Harry - b1957 Exeter NH dy
Sherri Lyn - b1963 Exeter NH

CHANDLER, Phil - m Marjorie Irma EVANS
Stuart Evans - b1951 Fitchburg MA
Bennett Russell - b1958 Boston MA
Peter Richards - b1959 Boston MA

CLARK, Jonnie S - m Vivian DeLong BROWN
Dawn - m Sam HOUSTON

CLARK, Lewis P - b1880 Nottingham NH m Martha Brown DRYSDALE
Joseph A - b1903 Hampton Falls NH m Marion Thompson no issue

CLARKE, Ronald L - b1935 Fall River MA m Merrell Gale WHEELOCK
Tammie Rae - b1959 Fall River MA
Peter - b1962 Fall River MA

CLINE, _____ m Diane Carolyn MORRISON
Tammy Ann - b1975
Clara Lynn - b1981

Descendant Chart

COLWELL, Richard Mowry - b1914 Woonsocket RI m Mary Jean RICHARDSON
    Cynthia Jean - b1951 Amherst MA
    Craig Richardson - b1953 Amherst MA
    Alyson Winsor - b1958 Bellafonte PA

CORREY, Larry Dean - b Perry IA m Gloria Alma SHEELY
    Christopher Lee - b1965
    Kathleen Mae - b1966

COULTER, Leslie Hamilton - m Shirley Ann BROWN
    Kevin James - b1965 Springfield MA
    Jeffrey Allen - b1966 Springfield MA
    Amy Lynn - b1968 Springfield MA

CRONIN, Frederick Arthur - b1949 Amesbury MA m Margaret Jean WHITE
    Frederick Arthur - b1968 Amesbury MA

DEARBORN, George Edwin - b1893 Exeter NH m Jennie Mae BURKE
    Priscilla - b1922 Exeter NH m Francis Mitchell WALSH
    George Edwin - b1918 Exeter NH n Joyce Louisa Roberts
    Sandra - b1953 Ft Worth TX

DEARBORN, George James - bc1860 Hampton NH m Agnes Jane WHENAL
    Mabel Josephine - b1890 Hampton NH m Harry Clinton MARSTON
    Godfrey Milton - b1891 Hampton NH m Anna Kruger
        Norman Milton - b1917 Exeter NH m Henrietta E Chase no issue
        Elsie Edith - b1922 Exeter NH m Paul Philip Thurlow
    Martha J - unm

DEARBORN (Continued)
    Marian G - m Clement Newton AYERS

DELUDE, Richard - m Dawn Lind McDONOUGH
    Kerry Lynne - b1968 Dover NH m Carl David Ashburn
    David Allan - b1974 Dover NH

DONATELLO, George Victor - b1944 Manchuria m Mary Louise WALSH
    Jeffrey George - b1968 Canal Zone
    James Andrew - b1971 Lincoln Park NJ

DOWNING, Clayton Woodbury - b1946 Exeter NH m Carla Lind BURKLUND
    Clinton Tod - b1965 Zion IL
    Correy Lee - b1966 Norfolk VA
    Christa Lynn - b1967 Kittery ME

DROWN, Richard E - m Robin Leigh BURKLUND
    Lauren Amy - b1982 Rochester NH

DRYSDALE, Joseph - b1846 Scotland m Mary Ann BROWN
    William - b1867 Scotland m Margaret I Cannon
        Walter James - b1901 Rye NH m Fanny Jenness Towle
        Jeannie Maricanne - b1903 North Hampton NH unm
        Jessie Dodge - b1906 North Hampton NH m Irving Knight STROUT
        John William - b1909 North Hampton NH m Minnie Mae Eugley no issue
        Margaret Isabella - b1918 North Hampton NH m Earl Leslie BARKER
    Mary M. - b1870 Scotland m Stephen W ROWE
    Martha Brown - b1874 Hampton Falls NH m Lewis P CLARK

Descendant Chart

DRYSDALE (Continued)

Margaret D - b1875 Hampton Falls NH m Myron I EVANS
John - b1878 Hampton Falls NH m Annie Laurie Emery
Wallace Everett - b1901 Hampton NH m Vasilike Koukos
Paul John - b1949 Jackson Heights LI NY m Lynn Pezzica
Paul James - b1971
Sultana Marina - b1957 Jackson Heights LI NY
Annie F - b1887 Hampton Falls NH m Oscar H Johnson

DUARTE, Louis - m Joyce Adele BROWN
Donna Lee - bc1967 Central Falls RI m Jerry Scott
Lisa Louise - b1969 Central Falls RI

ESTABROOK, Kenneth I - b1926 m Bernice Arlene BROWN
Vivian Jean - b1944 Bridgeport CT m Edward J SOARES

EVANS, Myron Isaac - b1875 Londonderry NH m Margaret D DRYSDALE
Reginald Louis - b Londonderry NH m1 _____ m2 Anita _____
Richard - child by 1st wife
Oliver Drysdale - b1898 Londonderry NH m Margaret _____ no issue
Sheridan Blodgett - b1900 Londonderry NH m1 Edna Coombs no issue m2 Ethel Strid
Barbara - m Pierre Topps
Russell Myron - b1901 Derry NH m Irma Alice Rogers
Alice Elizabeth - b1925 White Plains NY m Victor E HUDON
Marjorie Irma - b1929 Nashua NH m Phil CHANDLER
Louise Rogers - b1932 Nashua NH m Leonard E BUSSIERE

EWING, Norman S - b1908 Woodland ME m Marion Beatrice BROWN

131

EWING (Continued)
  Thomas Brown - b1934 Portsmouth NH m Jane Audre Porter
    Thomas Brown - b1960 Framingham MA
    Robert Scott - b1964 Tolland CT
    Lynn E - b1954 Manchester NH (adopted)

FARRINGTON, John J - b1946 m Sonjia Lee CARTER
  Robert William - b1968 Exeter NH

FERRY, Lawrence Joseph - b1921 Assonett MA m Dorothy May WHEELOCK
  Lawrence Joseph - b1946 Fall River MA m Janice Diane Perry
    Leslie Janice - b1968 Fall River MA
    Lawrence Joseph - b1969 Fall River MA
  Gary Francis - b1953 Fall River MA
  Gail Marie - b1963 Fall River MA

FRANCIS, Donald - b1933 McKinley ME m Beverly A WHENAL
  David Alan - b1960 Glendale CA
  Robert Michael - b1961 Glendale CA
  James Andrew - b1966 Glendale CA

FULLER, Dale Russell - m Judith April PAIGE
  Kaleena April - b1982
  Keith Ernest - b1984
  Zachary Russell - b1985

GALFORD, Bert - m Joan Ann WHEELOCK
  Craig Michael - b1964

GALFORD (Continued)
    Kevin Thomas - b1965
    Keith James - b1967

GERNT, Richard L - m Linda Louise HOITT
    Bruce Richard - b1961 Orlando FL
    Lisa Lynn - b1962 Orlando FL

GOODWIN, David M - m Sharon Louise LANE
    David M - b1962
    Brenda Lynn - b1963
    Tracy - b1965
    Richard Allan - b1967

GRANT, Gordon Wilson - b1926 Exeter NH m Marilyn Frances WHENAL
    Gail Marie - b1961 Exeter NH

GRAVES, Thomas Henry - b1911 Amherst NH m Florence WHENAL
    Malcom John - b1936 Exeter NH m Marie Mahar
        Diane Helen - b1957 Exeter NH
        Malcom John - b1960 Exeter NH
        Steven Lee - b1962 Exeter NH
    Lloyd Thomas - b1937 Exeter NH

HARGER, George - b1931 m Susan Amy LEACH
    Gretchen Stephanie - b1966 Springfield MA
    Kristine Amy - b1969 Springfield MA

Descendant Chart

HOBBS, John Oliver - b1822 Exeter NH m Isabella Marilyn WHENAL
 Linda Christine - b1948 Exeter NH m Terry O'Connor

HOITT, Clarence Harrison - b1880 Portsmouth NH m1 Dora Elizabeth BROWN m2 Alice _____
 Clarence Brown - b1901 Portsmouth NH m1 Rheta Lois Williams m2 Helen (Wilson) Metz no issue
 Harrison Heffenger - b1901 Portsmouth NH m1 Ruth Tilton 2 ch m2 Mary Alice Gifford 4 ch
  Frank Bartlett -
  June Rose -
  Scott Gifford - b1929 Portsmouth NH m1 Jean Lois MacMasters 1 ch m2 Nancy E Henderson
   Donna Lee - b1954 Portsmouth NH m1 James J KELLY m2 L Scot Folensbee m3 Stephen LEIGHTON
   Michael Scott - b1966 Portsmouth NH (adopted)
    Catherine - bc1976 (adopted)
  Palmer Brent - b1932 Portsmouth NH dy
  Gayle Ardelle - b1933 Portsmouth NH m1 Salvatore Alosa m2 Robert Sherman WOODBURN
  Linda Louise - b1939 Concord NH m1 Richard L GERNT m2 Joseph Charles Lewis
  Ernest -
  Edward -

HOUSTON, Sam - m Dawn CLARK
 Jason Lee - b1980 Carthage MS

HUDON, Victor E - m Alice Elizabeth EVANS
 Michael Evans - b1950 Nashua NH
 Anne Victoria - b1951 Nashua NH

JAFFERY, Richard - m Janet Constance MARBLE
 Robert Charles - b1984

Descendant Chart

JENNESS, Samuel Alonzo - b1844 North Hampton NH m Martha BROWN
    George W - b1875 North Hampton NH m Etta French no issue
    Florence May - b1878 North Hampton NH m Harrison W TYLER
    Newell C - b1880 North Hampton NH m Nellie I Wentworth
        Viola May - b1906 North Andover MA m Merton PITKIN
        Hazel Irene - b1907 North Andover MA m Clayton Vernon PITKIN
    Clara E - b1883 North Hampton NH m Elmer Austin BERRY

JORGENSEN, Jay Keith - m Gail Paige Patricia METZE
    Kimberly - b1963 MN
    Joni - b1966 MN

KELLY, James Joseph - m Donna Lee HOITT
    Bradley James - b1975 Exeter NH

LAFFEY, Joseph - m Marian Virginia AYERS
    Scot David - b1953 Jamaica Plains MA
    Martha Jane - b1954 Jamaica Plains MA

LAMB, Donald - b1939 Providence RI m Sheryl Lee WHEELOCK
    Shelly Ann - b1967 Fall River MA
    Christopher Paul - b1971 Fall River MA

LANE, Howard M - b1870 Hampton NH m Lydia May WHENAL
    Beatrice Merrill - b1909 Hampton NH m Eugene M Leavitt no issue
    Herman W - b1911 Hampton NH m Lillian Littlefield
        Herman W - b1932 Newburyport MA m Barbara Neil no issue
        Robert - b1938 Hampton NH m Marieanne Severence no issue

LANE (Continued)
    Sharon Louise - b1943 Exeter NH m David M GOODWIN
    Charles William - b1946 Exeter NH m Carol Ann Allen

LEACH, Clifford - m Glady Richmond BARTON
    Barton Brayley - b1933 New Bedford MA m Ruth Smith
        Brenda - b1959
        Nancy - b1962
        Dana - b1966
    Jane Holdsworth - b 1935 New Bedford MA m David Fisher SWEET
    Susan Amy - b1938 New Bedford MA m George HARGER

LEIGHTON, Roger Stephen b1950 Concord NH m Donna Lee HOITT
    Kate Allison - b1986 Exeter NH
    Ashley Joy - b1988 Exeter NH

LONG, William - m Penny Lou PITKIN
    Christopher William - b1974 Exeter NH
    Melissa - b1979 Exeter NH

McDONOUGH, Leo Francis - b1917 Concord NH m Ruth Irma BUZZELL
    Maureen Frances - b1940 Northwood NH m Norman Lawrence POMEROY
    Dawn Lind - b1949 Exeter NH m Richard DELUDE

MARBLE, Leonard Joseph - b1918 Haverhill MA m Barbara Maynes BROWN
    Thomas Howard - b1952 Haverhill MA m Diana Illsley
    Janet Constance - b1954 Haverhill MA m Richard JAFFERY

Descendant Chart

MARDEN, Linwood Eric - m Debbie Lee BURKLUND
  Linwood Eric - b1977 Concord NH
  Jessica Lee -

MARKIE, Richard Patrick - m Deborah Ann STANDISH
  Heather Leigh - b1970 Exeter NH
  Derek Richard - b1975 Exeter NH

MARSTON, Harry Clinton - b1883 North Hampton NH m Mabel Josephine DEARBORN
  Curtis Dearborn - b1914 North Hampton NH m Louise Webb
    Alan Curtis - b1940 Newburyport MA m Barbara Ann Hood
      Leisa Ann - b1960 Exeter NH
      Gordon Curtis - b1961 Exeter NH dy
      Michael Alan - b1963 Exeter NH
    Paul Stuart - b1943 Exeter NH m Mary Guerrera
      Curtis Anthony - b1966 Exeter NH
      Paul Joseph - b1968 Exeter NH

MESERVE, Robert Harold - m Piper Alayne PAIGE
  Adam Robert - b1980 Dover NH
  Erin Paige - b1981 Dover NH

METZE, George Martin - b1918 Chicago IL m Hazel Shirley Mary WHEELOCK
  Gail Paige Patricia - b1941 Fall River MA m Jay Keith JORGENSEN
  George Martin - b1949 Newport RI

MILLS, Leroy - b Fall River MA m Shirley WHEELOCK
  Geoffrey Scott - b1961 Fall River MA

Descendant Chart

MILLS (Continued)
    Lori Ann - b1963 Fall River MA

MORRISON, Oscar - b1866 Canada m Jennie Whenal BROWN
    Lillian Ardelle - b1895 dy
    Oscar Linwood - b1899 Exeter NH m Pauline Vivian Hobbs
        Bradford Hobbs - b1925 Kittery ME m Carolyn Jean Mathews
            Dean Bradford - b1949 Portland ME
            Diane Carolyn - b1952 Portland ME m _____ CLINE
            Sandra Dawn - b1962 Waltham MA
            Penny Jean - b1964 Stamford CT
    Helen Fern - b1900 Exeter NH m Victor M Mitchell no issue

NELSON, William H - b Boston MA m Anne Elizabeth WHENAL
    Catherine Anne - b1957 Portsmouth NH

OSGOOD, Charles - b1868 Fremont NH m Elizabeth Campbell BROWN
    Carroll William - b1890 Brentwood NH m1 Bessie Bell Ham m2 Blanche Sanborn no issue

PAIGE, Walter Vincent - b1925 Long Island NY m Marlene Adelaide BURKLUND
    Heidi Allyn - b1955 Dover NH m Daniel ROBIDAS
    Peter Alan - b1956 Dover NH
    Piper Alayne - b1957 Rochester NH m Robert Harold MESERVE
    Darin Andrew - b1959 Rochester NH
    Jill Alana - b1960 Rochester NH m Jeffrey Allen SHERWOOD
    son - b1962 Rochester NH dy
    Jeffrey Adam - b1965 Dover NH twin
    Judith April - b1965 Dover NH twin m Dale Russell FULLER

PAIGE (Continued)
Jennifer Ann - b1968 Dover NH

PITKIN, Clayton Vernon - b Haverhill MA m Hazel Irene JENNESS
Harlan Le Roy - b1926 Haverhill MA m Audrey DeFoe
Kenneth Frederick - b1948 Kennebunk ME m Veronica Bolduc
Mathew Kenneth - b1972 Exeter NH
Mark - b1974
Elaine Viola - b1949 Biddeford ME m Walter C Glover
Albert Harlan - b1951 Exeter NH
Donna Lee - b1952 Exeter NH m Arthur G ROLLINS
Eunice Carlene - b1953 Exeter NH
Marie Ann - b1954 Exeter NH
Penny Lou - b1958 Exeter NH m William LONG
Tina - b1968
Frederick Elmer - b1928 Haverhill MA m Olive Beatrice Dusheimin
Pamela Jean - b Haverhill MA m Robert W Ryan
Frederick Elmer - b Haverhill MA m Victoria Keir
Stephanie Eve - b1972 Exeter NH

PITKIN, Merton - b1905 Haverhill MA m Viola May JENNESS
Newell Vernon - b1925 Merrimac MA m Gloria G (Batchelder) Barrett
Gerard Newell - b1955 Exeter NH m Anne C Haberski
Matthew Gerard - b1980 Haverhill MA
Ronald Robert - b1956 Exeter NH m Cheryl-Ann Borin
Richard Jenness - b1960 Haverhill MA
?Patty - m _____ Perrault
Shirley Elaine - b1929 Merrimac MA unm

Descendant Chart

POMEROY, Norman Lawrence - m Maureen Frances McDONOUGH
    Michael Francis - b1960 Portsmouth NH (adopted)
    Shawn Patrick - b1964 Dover NH

PORTER, Harold Carey - m Mabel Faith BROWN
    Doris Brown - b1921 Newburyport MA m Arthur BASTINE

PRENTISS, Arthur Russell - b1933 Manchester NH m Judith Lee BROWN
    Linda Lee - b1953 Manchester NH
    David Scott - b1956 Manchester NH
    Mark Wallace - b1966 Manchester NH
    Lisa June - b1970 Manchester NH

PURINGTON, Ira C - b1867 Epping NH m Elizabeth Campbell BROWN
    Ethel - dy

REID, Hartwell Berry - b1898 Amesbury MA m Isabell Wiseman BROWN
    James Elliott - b1924 Newburyport MA m Lorraine M Geoffrey
        James Elliott - b1948 Amesbury MA
        Thomas Alan - b1950 Amesbury MA m Michele D'Alessandro
            Lisa Michele - 1970 Haverhill MA
        Bonnie Elizabeth - b1953 Amesbury MA
        Linda Jean - b Amesbury MA

RICHARDSON, Douglas Josiah - b1900 Nova Scotia m Mary Isabelle WHEELOCK
    Helen Susan - b1924 Fall River MA m Robert Charles CARD
    Mary Jean - b1925 Fall River MA m Richard Mowry COLWELL
    Douglas Josiah - b1933 Fall River MA m Myrna Evans

RICHARDSON (Continued)
    Beth Ann - b1956 Weymouth MA
    Douglas Josiah - b1958 Quincy MA
    Stephanie - b1960 Meriden CT
    Mary Susan - b1962 Boston MA

ROBIDAS, Daniel m Heidi Allyn PAIGE
    Alan Daniel - b1980 Dover NH
    Andrew George - b1981 Dover NH

ROESSLER, Paul - m Bonnie Susan AJEMIAN
    Tracey Allison - b1973 Exeter NH

ROLLINS, Arthur G - m Donna Lee PITKIN
    Jason Arthur - b1971 Exeter NH
    Abbi Audrey-Grace - b1978 Exeter NH

ROSE, Howard - b1907 Acushnet MA m Isabel Brown BARTON
    Francis Eugene - b1937 New Bedford MA m Barbara E George no issue

ROWE, Stephen W - b1866 Seabrook NH m Mary M DRYSDALE
    Stephen - unm

SANTOSUOSSO, Michael G - b1927 South Hampton NH m Deanna Frances WHITE
    Michael G - b1961 Amesbury MA
    David James - b1962 Amesbury MA
    Sharon Lee - b1964 Amesbury MA
    Sheila Ann - b1966 Amesbury MA

SAWYER, Glenn W - b1911 West Medway MA m Verna E BERRY
    Kenneth - b1940 Milford MA m Mary Lou Francis
        Tisha Lee Frances - b1969 Worcester MA

SCHMITT, Francis Louis - b1933 Buffalo NY m Sylvia Louise WHENAL
    Timothy Thomas - b1958 Buffalo NY
    Karen Louise - b1959 Buffalo NY
    Susan Marie - b1961 Buffalo NY
    Stephen Francis - b1962 Buffalo NY

SHEELY, Boucher - m Alma G TYLER
    Gloria Alma - b1941 Evansville IN m Larry Dean CORREY
    Ross Edward - b1943 Evansville IN m Flo _____

SHERWOOD, Jeffrey Allen - m Jill Alana PAIGE
    David -
    Karlie Alana - b1982 Dover NH

SILVIA, Richard William - b1945 Fall River MA m Linda Sue CARD
    Michael William - b1970 Plainfield NJ

SIMPSON, Robert Henry - b1929 Dover NH m Ruth Irma BUZZELL
    Robert Henry - b1955 Exeter NH m Ann Marie Caswell
        Justin -

SOARES, Edward J - b1940 Fall River MA m Vivian Jean ESTABROOK
    JoAnn - b1964 Pawtucket RI
    Michael Edward - b1965 Pawtucket RI

SOARES (Continued)
   Denise Marie - b1970 Pawucket RI

STANDISH, Dwight Amos - b1909 Exeter NH m Beatrice May BROWN
   Gordon Amos - b1928 Exeter NH m Mary Elizabeth Rusine
      Deborah Ann - b1949 Exeter NH m Richard Patrick MARKIE
         Alan Gordon - b1952 Exeter NH
         Brenda Mae - b1958 Exeter NH m Stephen A Haslam
         Mark William - b1963 Exeter NH

      Elaine - stillborn
      son - stillborn 1932

STROUT, Irving Knight - b1897 Bradford ME m Jessie Dodge DRYSDALE
   Irving Knight - b1930 Newburyport MA m Phyllis Ann Rich
      Karen Ann - b1956 Exeter NH
      Steven Lee - b1959 Exeter NH
   George Andrew - b1936 Hampton NH m Mary Ann Palmer
      George Andrew - b1962 Columbus OH
      Douglas Michael - b1964 Albany NY

SWEET, David Fisher - b1934 m Jane Holdsworth LEACH
   Jennifer - b1960
   Elizabeth - b1962 triplet
   David Fisher - b1962 triplet
   William - b 1962 triplet

TOWLE, Gerald Charles - b1912 Fremont NH m Wilma Lois BUZZELL
   Laird Charles - b1933 Exeter NH m Marlene Ann Towne

TOWLE (Continued)
  Karen Lee - b1957 Exeter NH m Nicholas John George Ackermann
  Joel Andrew - b1960 Charlottesville VA
  Glenn Corbett - b1962 Exeter NH m Michele Mollick
  Leslie Kim - b1965 Milwaukee WI

TROTTA, Joseph - m Janet Elaine BLATCHFORD
  Stephen Joseph - b1976 Exeter NH

TYLER, Harrison W - b1878 Kensington NH m Florence May JENNESS
  Wilbur H - b1901 m but no issue
  Mary Gertrude - b1902 North Hampton NH m1 Ross Barnett m2 Clark Smell no issue
  Newell Basil - b1904 Hampton NH dy
  Lester Jenness - b1906 North Hampton NH m but no issue
  Alma G - b1911 Amesbury MA m1 Boucher SHEELY m2 Ernest Suihkonen

WALSH, Francis Mitchell - b1920 Newington NH m Priscilla DEARBORN
  William Mitchell - b1942 Exeter NH m Paula Somerville
    Christopher Dearborn - b1966 Exeter NH
    Amy Elizabeth - bc1969 Melrose MA
  Mary Louise - b1945 Exeter NH m George Victor DONATELLO
  Linda Dearborn - b1948 Exeter NH m James C Cavenaugh
  Laurel Jane - b1949 Exeter NH m William Bradley Patterson

WELLS, Carlton L - b1890 Amesbury MA m Lena Jane BROWN
  Virginia E - b1923 Philadelphia PA (adopted)

WHEELOCK, William North - b1863 Nova Scotia m Isabella BROWN

WHEELOCK (Continued)

Andrew Leroy - b1884 Hampton Falls NH m1 Florence May Kimber 2 ch m2 Susan M Wing no issue

    Florence Isabel - b1906

    William Major - b1907 Fall River MA m Pauline Gadsby

        Kimber Gadsby - b1933 Fall River MA m1 Elizabeth Lancaster no issue m2 Patricia Lee Nero

            Jessica Nero - b1968 Wakefield RI

    Major William - b1887 Fall River MA m Sadie Pierce

        North William - b1918 Fall River MA m Jean Buffington

            Merrell Gale - b1940 m Ronald L CLARKE

            North William - b1943 unm

            Sheryl Lee - b1944 m Donald L AMB

            Peter Loring - b1947 unm

            Jeanne Suzanne - b1954

            Jill Ann -

    Donald Thomas - b Fall River MA m Thelma Scholes

        Joan Ann - b1943 m Bert GALFORD

        Donald Thomas - b1944 m Barbara Soares

            Barry Peter - b1950

            Mary Lou - b1955

            Lynn - b1960

    Loring Russell - b1927 Fall River MA m Betty Gable

        Karen - b1955 Fall River MA

Frank Norman - b1889 Fall River MA m1 Gertrude Wilson 8 ch m2 Susan M (Wing) Wheelock no issue

    Marion Gertrude - b1913 Fall River MA m Frederick Wesley no issue

    Frankly Edward - b1914 Fall River MA m Margaret Whetstine

        Gary Edward - b1939

        Gerald Jay - b1942

        Wesley Andrew - b1945

145

Descendant Chart

WHEELOCK (Continued)
    Major William - b1916 Fall River MA m Mildred Rogers
        Major William - b1936 Fall River MA m Rita Gauthier
            Major William - b1963 Washington DC
            Nancy Beth - b1967 Silver Spring MD
        Shirley - b1939 Fall River MA m Leroy MILLS
        Frank Norman - b1942 Fall River MA m Aline Rogers
            Frank Norman - b1965
    Andrew Leroy - b1917 Fall River MA m Jessie Wood no issue
    Ernest - b Fall River MA dy
    Hazel Shirley Mary - b1921 Fall River MA m George Martin METZE
    Wesley Barry - b1923 Fall River MA m Helen Newbury
        Wesley Barry - b1945 m Nancy Ferris
            Wesley Barry - b1970
    Dorothy May - b1926 Fall River MA m Lawrence Joseph FERRY
    Jennie May - b1891 Fall River MA m1 Robert BARTON m2 Albert L BRALEY
    Mary Isabel - b1900 Fall River MA m Douglas Josiah RICHARDSON

WHENAL, William - b1836 Scotland m Jane BROWN
    Robert - b1865 Scotland unm
    Agnes Jane - b1867 Scotland m George James DEARBORN
    John - b1869 Scotland m Carrie Augusta Marston
    infant - dy
        Martin Wade - b1904 North Hampton NH m Hazel Varney
        John Leslie - b1928 Portsmouth NH m Shirley Marston
            Beverly - b1958 Manchester NH
            Bruce - b1961 Manchester NH
        John Winthrop - b1907 North Hampton NH dy

146

WHENAL (Continued)

Augusta Evelyn - b1911 North Hampton NH unm
John William - b1918 North Hampton NH m Hazel Lovett
Rev Barry - b1947 Exeter NH Episcopal Priest
Thomas Benjamin - b1871 North Hampton NH m Isabella J White
Harry Thomas - b1895 Rye NH m Charlotte E Taylor
Milton W - b1930 Exeter NH m Beverly Jean Spear
Stuart Wesley - b1955 Beverly MA
Scott Frederick - b1959 Beverly MA
Shaun Alda - b1962 Beverly MA
Robyn Bryne - b1970 Beverly MA
Anne Elizabeth - b1931 m1 Arnold BRAYALL m2 William H NELSON
Helen Ferdelia - b1897 North Hampton NH m Clarence M Shrock
George Earle - b1902 North Hampton NH m Esther Lillian Blaney
Isabella Marilyn - b1925 North Hampton NH m John Oliver HOBBS
Gloria Ruth - b1928 Kittery ME m George AJEMIAN
Marilyn Frances - b1930 Kittery ME m Gordon Wilson GRANT
Josephine W - b1904 North Hampton NH dy
William Teele - b1908 North Hampton NH m Katherine R Christie
William Teele - b1934 Rockport MA m Carol Burton
dau
Beverly A - b1935 Exeter NH m Donald FRANCIS
Sylvia Louise - b1936 Exeter NH m Francis Louis SCHMITT
Florence - b1915 North Hampton NH m Thomas Henry GRAVES
Sarah Belle - b1874 North Hampton NH m Frank Coffin no issue
Louis C - b1877 North Hampton NH d ae 19 unm
Lydia May - b1879 North Hampton NH m Howard LANE

WHITE, Thomas Bush - b1890 Amesbury MA m Ella Margaret BROWN
Mabel Frances - b1914 Amesbury MA m1 Roland M Frye m2 Paul Hurst no issue
James Goodrich - b1916 Amesbury MA m Helen Joanne Brozewich
Deanna Frances - b1937 Amesbury MA m Michael G SANTOSUOSSO
John Thomas - b1944 Amesbury MA m Janet M Lawrie
Thomas Bush - b1919 Amesbury MA m Muriel E Evans
Glenda Ruth - b1943 Amesbury MA m Michael Schneider
Carole Anne - b1947 Amesbury MA
Margaret Jean - b1948 Amesbury MA m Frederick Arthur CRONIN
Thomas David - b1949 Amesbury MA

WOODBURN, Robert Sherman - b1933 Methuen MA m Gayle Ardelle HOITT
Nancy Lee - b1959 Exeter NH m Neil Joseph Pendergast
Robert David - b1961 Exeter NH

INDEX

This index covers all names in the book, except those in the Scottish Gazetteer chapter.

Index

Index

Index

154

Index

Index

Index

Index

Index

Heritage Books by Wilma T. Regan and Laird C. Towle:

*The Descendants of William Brown (1819–1908) and Isabella Kennedy
(1820–1894) of Ireland, Scotland, and Hampton Falls, New Hampshire*

Heritage Books by Laird C. Towle:

Genealogical Periodical Annual Index series:

Volume 13 (1974)–Volume 25 (1986)
Leslie K. Towle and Laird C. Towle

Volume 26 (1987)
Karen T. Ackermann and Laird C. Towle

Volume 27 (1988)
Leslie K. Towle and Laird C. Towle

Volume 28 (1989)
Leslie K. Towle and Laird C. Towle

Volume 30 (1991)–Volume 31 (1992)
Leslie K. Towle and Laird C. Towle

Volume 33 (1994)
Leslie K. Towle and Laird C. Towle

Volume 38 (1999)–Volume 39 (2000)
Leslie K. Towle and Laird C. Towle

Volume 40 (2001)
Karen T. Ackermann and Laird C. Towle, Ph.D.

Volume 41 (2002)
Karen T. Ackermann and Laird C. Towle, Ph.D.

New England Annals, Volume 1: History and Genealogy

New Hampshire Genealogical Research Guide
Laird C. Towle, Ph. D. and Ann N. Brown

www.ingramcontent.com/pod-product-compliance
Lightning Source LLC
Chambersburg PA
CBHW061734270326
41928CB00011B/2227